Don't worry about where the buck stops, learn where the buck starts.

Copyright 2007 - Wayne Ahart
Published by Lulu.com

All rights reserved. No part of this book may be reproduced in any form without permission in writing from the author except by a reviewer who wishes to quote brief passages in connection wtih a review written for inclusion in a magazine, newspaper, or other informational media. Proper credits required.

First edition 2007

Printed in the United States of America

ISBN: 978-1-4303-2076-0

# YES!
## You CAN Become A Millionaire

*By Wayne E. Ahart*

*Winning the lottery, striking oil, mining gold, inheriting riches are quicker ways to wealth. If you're not likely to experience these, the success formula outlined in this book is for you!*

### How To Break The Success Code!

My Mom and Dad were sharecroppers, yet,
I learned the formula that enabled me to earn millions.
If you want to learn what I learned, read this book!
If you're not interested - save your time.

Don't worry about where the buck stops,
learn where the buck starts.

# DEDICATION

Inspiration is a wonderful thing and there are various ways to attain it.

- Encouragement by people who believe in you and whom you believe in can be a great source of inspiration.
- Starting with nothing and wanting to make something of yourself is a source of inspiration.
- Believing in yourself is inspirational.
- Knowledge is inspirational.
- Seeing others achieve greatness is inspirational.
- Love of country is inspirational.
- A truly strong faith is inspirational.
- Love of work is inspirational.
- Freedom is inspirational.
- Opportunity is inspirational.

If you are inspired enough and perspire enough, any goal can be achieved.

I dedicate this book to all my friends, acquaintances and

business associates who, through the years, have inspired me by one or more of these means. There are hundreds who will not be mentioned here, but I know who they are and they know who they are.

There are a few I must mention:

My Mom and Dad inspired me in uncountable ways, but in particular by their love for each other and all the family. I was inspired by their faith, their work ethic, and uncompromising honesty.

My sister and seven brothers were just extensions of Mom and Dad and for my 67 years have been a source of support and inspiration. Special note to my brother, Tom Ahart, who noticed when I was a teen that I had a lazy sauntering style of walking. After a good lecture about the nature of a brisk, enthusiastic way of walking (complete with his demonstration), I heeded his advice and became a walker that demonstrated that I was busy, knew where I was going and in a hurry to get there. Thanks, Tom!

I have five children and four grandsons. I cannot begin to describe the many times and events in which they inspired me, taught me and made me proud! Wow, what a crew!

My children: Deborah Ahart Berman, Indianapolis, Indiana; Lance, Oklahoma City, Oklahoma; Doug, Christopher and Kevin, all of Austin, Texas.

My grandsons: Max and Karl Berman, Indianapolis, Indiana; Pierce and Reeves Ahart, Austin, Texas.

Thanks to two former bosses, Doyle Venable, owner of Venable Lumber Company in North Little Rock, Arkansas and D.N. "Nick" Pope, founder of National Foundation Life Insurance Company, Oklahoma City, Oklahoma and other companies.

Both of these gentlemen were more than my boss. They were my friend, they treated me almost like a son and both spent time training me and inspiring me. Both were hard drivers, positive thinkers, goal-oriented, patriotic Americans and men of integrity.

One's success is often determined by the people he/she surrounds themselves with. In this event, I have been truly blessed.

- Barry Shamas, Executive Vice President and Chief Operating Officer of Brokers National Life Assurance Company (BNL). Barry has been a Godsend. He is a CPA, graduated Magna Cum Laude and is one of the very smartest men I have been around. Top that off with rock solid integrity and a streak of fearlessness and you'll see why he has been an inspiration to me. Barry and I have been associated for 38 years.
- Don Byrd and Kenny Tobey. I have seen both of these men grow from nothing to outstanding leaders. Don is Vice Chairman and Kenny is President of BNL. Their integrity, their work ethic, their enthusiasm and competitiveness assured their climb from an agent's position to their current Executive positions. Working with them and watching them has been inspirational. Don has been associated with us for 33 years and Kenny for 26 years. They work with approximately 5,000 agents and insurance brokers in 40 states.

BNL has numerous other inspirational officers and/or supervisors that have been with the Company over 20 years due to the leadership qualities of Barry, Don and Kenny.

I have received great inspiration from each and every member of the Board of Directors of the life insurance companies I have been privileged to serve as chairman.

- Serving on these boards were former governors, congressmen,

mayors, a university president, five Hall of Fame collegiate football coaches, and an NFL Hall of Fame coach (Super Bowl winner), president of National Cattlemen's Association, National Pork Producers Council, Executive Secretary of same, National Livestock and Meat Board, United States Secretary of Agriculture, bankers, three past presidents and/or chairmen of American Truckers Association, two former State Securities Commissioners, a former state insurance commissioner, a president of a state medical association, and an astronaut who left the last footprint on the moon.
- Literally hundreds of other community leaders across the states of Indiana, Nebraska, Texas, Iowa, Arkansas and Tennessee.
- In addition, a small group of dedicated Americans in Bee Cave, Texas, my breakfast buddies. Philosophy majors all (without the diploma), inspired by their leader T. Boothe. A mixed bag of leaders in varied fields who have been inspirational and entertaining. We meet at Jim Bob's BBQ.
- A preacher, golfing buddy and true friend, Rex D. Johnson of Austin, Texas. Reverend Rex and wife Patti took over a small church of approximately 55-60 members in 1990. They have since built two buildings and have a current membership of 1,400.

Rex and his family (outstanding singers) are inspiring in many ways. It is particularly inspirational when I beat him in golf. It is also seldom, I might add. He's good!
- And to Christie Smith, a capable and valued member of BNL's Marketing Department who convinced me this should be published and took the ball and ran with it.

It is to all these great people who served to inspire me, I dedicate this book. (See list of Board Members immediately following).

Board of Directors in the companies I have formed:

| | | |
|---|---|---|
| C. James McCormick | Indiana | *President, American Trucking Association* |
| | | *Resort developer* |
| Earl Butz | Indiana | *Former Secretary of Agriculture* |
| Chris Schenkel | Indiana | *ABC Sports commentator* |
| Dr. John Ryan | Indiana | *President, Indiana University* |
| Mike Kinney | Indiana | *Real estate* |
| George Doane | Indiana | *Attorney* |
| Dr. William Elliott, MD | Indiana | *Cardiologist* |
| George Morton | Indiana | *Farmer* |
| Samuel H. Washburn | Indiana | *Cattle* |
| Herb Albers, Jr. | Nebraska | *Cattle* |
| Dr. Warren Bosley, MD | Nebraska | *President, Nebraska Medical Association* |
| Merlyn Carlson | Nebraska | *President, National Cattlemen's Association* |
| Coach Bob Devaney | Nebraska | *Nebraska Cornhuskers, Hall of Fame* |
| Senator E.T. Johnson | Nebraska | *Cattle / State Senator* |
| Steve Sutherlin | Indiana | *Attorney - State Securities Commissioner* |
| Governor Charles Thone | Nebraska | *Governor / Former Congressman* |
| Robert Simmons | Nebraska | *Attorney* |
| Robert L. Bliss | Texas | *Cattle* |
| Mac O. Boring, Jr. | Texas | *Oil drilling* |
| Coach Frank Broyles | Arkansas | *University of Arkansas Razorbacks, Hall of Fame* |
| Captain Eugene Cernan | Texas | *Astronaut - two moon missions* |
| Robert H. Cutler | Texas | *President, American Trucking Association* |
| William M. King | Texas | *Attorney - Texas Securities Commissioner* |
| Coach Tom Landry | Texas | *Dallas Cowboys, Hall of Fame* |

| | | |
|---|---|---|
| Coach Darrell Royal | Texas | Texas Longhorns, Hall of Fame |
| Stoney M. Stubbs | Texas | President, American Trucking Association |
| Otis S. West | Texas | Banker / King Ranch Executive |
| Coach Hayden Fry | Iowa | Iowa Hawkeyes, Hall of Fame |
| Roy Keppy | Iowa | Farmer / President, National Pork Producers & National Livestock & Meat Board |
| Representative John Greig | Iowa | Cattle / State Representative |
| James Mullins | Iowa | Cattle / President, National Livestock & Meat Board |
| Robert Rigler | Iowa | Banker / State Senator / Chairman, Iowa Department of Transportation / Iowa Superintendent of Banking |
| Stanley Schoelerman | Iowa | Cattle / Director, Iowa Department of Transportation |
| Orville Sweet | Iowa | Executive Secretary, National Pork Producers / President, National Polled Hereford Association |
| Governor Winfield Dunn | Tennessee | Oral Surgeon / Governor |
| Mayor Richard Fulton | Tennessee | Former Congressman |
| Sam Bartholomew, Jr. | Tennessee | Attorney / National Director Vietnam Veterans |
| Coach Johnny Majors | Tennessee | Tennessee Volunteers / Hall of Fame |
| Timmons Treadwell III | Tennessee | Insurance executive |
| Mayor Willie Herenton | Tennessee | Memphis mayor |
| W. Neil Thomas, III | Tennessee | Attorney |
| Cecil Alexander | Arkansas | Former Speaker of House of Representatives |
| Rep. Richard Barclay | Arkansas | CPA / State Representative |
| Roy Ledbetter | Arkansas | Director, Highland Industrial Park |

| | | |
|---|---|---|
| Mahlon A. Martin | Arkansas | *Director, Rockefeller Foundation / Arkansas Department of Finance* |
| Representative John Miller | Arkansas | *Insurance - Real estate / Former Speaker of the House* |
| Senator Knox Nelson | Arkansas | *Oil / Senate Leader* |
| Bobby Hopper | Arkansass | *Ford Dealer / Chairman, Arkansas Highway Department* |

## FROM THE BEGINNING

Throughout history, all great achievements have come as the result of effort, expended to achieve the goal of an improved standard of living. The seeking of money or value to improve one's standing is a basic human instinct.

In prehistoric times – man hunted and foraged for food and shelter to survive as best they could. Eventually, they learned to make crude tools and use animals to help make their job easier and more efficient for the purpose of gain. Even today, primitive tribes in Africa are recognized as to their quality of life by the number of cattle they own. Their importance and position of honor is determined by their accumulation of assets. Their slight progress on their way to becoming civilized is driven by a desire for gain, honor and standing.

Many wars have been fought among countries and kingdoms to improve ones lot and standing in life by physically taking what others have accumulated.

Certain societies have opted to steal or take away the assets of others as opposed to creating value or wealth on their own. Kings – Hitler – the former Soviet Union – pirates – organized crime down to petty thieves – theft is their chosen way to gain a better standard of living and profits. However, most great achievements, i.e. the automobile – trains – trucks – airplanes – tractors – ships – telephone – electricity – textiles – modern medicine – insurance – construction – highways – radio and TV – computers – paper and thousands of other things have come about by motivated humans, creatively seeking ways to earn money in order to improve one's standard of living and standing in the community of ones' peers.

Our Creator put something inside of us to instinctively know that we should earn our keep, and to constantly strive for improvement – in much the same manner that new mothers know instinctively to nurse, love and protect their new baby. Animals and birds know instinctively what to do with their young and migratory birds know instinctively when and where to fly. Similarly, man knows he should grow and achieve.

The achievements of man in America have accelerated at a mind-numbing pace. It would take a thick book just to list all the technological achievements in less than 200 years, a mere twinkling of the eye when compared to the known history of humanity. The primary reasons for these vast human achievements are freedom, law and order and the "incentive" system.

Freedom and law and order gives humans the courage to dare, to dream, to do, without fear of capture, enslavement or government interference or hindrance. After freedom and law and order, one word can be credited for America's economic world leadership. Incentive! It's a demonstrated fact that we are not inherently smarter than the rest of the world.

In 1984, I visited Beijing and Shanghai, China. I visited communes where people lived in small primitive homes, had a poor diet and nothing but minimum necessities. In spite of their poor living conditions, it was clear that these were good-hearted, highly intelligent people. They were neat and clean, their homes were clean, the commune was orderly and they loved their children as much as anyone in the world. Why, in these times, were they living like this? The answer shouts itself back at you. They enjoy only one of the three necessary ingredients for success. They have law and order, but have neither freedom nor incentive. You can have no incentive where freedom is denied.

Taiwan clearly shows what those same people can achieve when incentive is introduced to them. In America, the seeds of tomorrow's economic engine and the dominant industry giants of tomorrow, are incubating even now in the hearts and minds of energetic, positive minded young people, who are free to dream, with incentive to do so.

Freedom unleashed a torrent of instinctive creative abilities and the desire to improve life for self and society.

We must remember that every great success which creates wealth for an entrepreneur, makes a lot of other people wealthy in the process and provides solid careers for many middle and lower income families. America needs promoters and more and more great success stories. The most important person in society, economically speaking, may be the so-called "promoter"; the risk-taker who jump starts new ventures and new ideas. New people becoming wealthy keep the wheels of opportunity turning for us all. These risk takers need to be encouraged, recognized, appreciated and honored. They are true heroes we cannot do without. Unfortunately, creativity, ingenuity and entrepreneurship are being attacked today from many corners and an attempt is being made to make anyone doing these things successfully, appear greedy and selfish.

This idea is promoted by people who believe in a socialist way of life and want all achievers to look bad in society – they believe that the assets of achievers should be redistributed to common man (a modern day form of thievery) espousing the theory that all people should be equal. This ignores the basic drive that creates all progress, the instinctive desire to improve and gain value for a better life (incentive) and the concept that wealth gained in a legal enterprise, idea or in any moral endeavor is a noble achievement.

My son, Chris, in his last year at the University of Texas' Masters Accounting Program, wrote an insightful paper for the graduate school of business. In it, he quotes Bruce A. Kirchhoff's writings entitled "Entrepreneurship Economics." In general, Kirchoff views the marketplace as being driven by innovation. Innovation brings about invention that creates a new commercial product or service, thus creating a new demand for goods and services. Kirchhoff quotes Joseph Schumpeter's perception that the economy consists of innovations that destroy the existing markets, which cause established firms with older products to decline. This establishes that it is the innovative entrepreneur who creates new demand by destroying existing markets.

David Birch's 1979 research study of employment in all U.S. firms from 1969 through 1976 conclude that small firms of 100 or fewer employees created 81% of the new jobs in America. Kirchhoff proposed the idea of Entrepreneurship Economics because...

- Entrepreneurs are the creators of wealth through innovation
- Entrepreneurs are responsible for most job growth

- Entrepreneurs provide a fair and equitable method of wealth redistribution.

My view is that Chris' report on Kirchhoff's writings is on target. However, the reason it is and the reason we have innovation and inventions is the incentive system wrapped around freedom and law and order.

However, government at all levels, seems to be doing all it can to destroy man's incentive to create, develop or grow by tax disincentives, regulations and the ever-present risk of lawsuits. Ever notice how governmental bodies, from local to state and federal, have gradually and continually eroded our freedoms, added more and more taxes on achievers and creators, and have enacted so many rules and regulations that a person couldn't read all of them in a whole adult lifetime? They design more and more programs which encourage whole segments of society to ignore their natural instinct to care for themselves and improve their life, in favor of accepting government handouts – handouts that government must first take from the achievers of society to give to the poor. In the name of kindness and fairness, government has helped to make them poor and guarantees they will always remain so. This creates disincentives for achievers and removes the urgency or desire of the poor to take care of themselves, or to do better. "A kept dog won't hunt anymore." There is no problem related to the poor that cannot be cured by education and opportunity. Too many people are encouraged to do nothing by the welfare state mentality and achievers are discouraged by a punishing tax and regulatory system.

Today, if you are a poor person who chooses not to accept government handouts and wishes to act on your natural instincts to provide for yourself, you may have very little food, sanitation, or shelter and be subject to the dangers of the street. But, if you rob, rape, or murder someone, you are provided shelter in pristine sanitary places, fed well, provided basketball courts, weight rooms, TV's, libraries and no real responsibilities. What's wrong with this picture?

If America is to avoid economic collapse, it must reinstate the freedoms and boundless opportunities of early America – remove the yoke of limitless government regulations, which will release the creativity and ingenuity of her people again. Government regulations are well meaning but often misguided. Every regulation is based on the premise that government knows best. The results are predictable. It took two years to build my home in 1994. It only took 14 months to build the Empire state building in 1930.

Government must understand that life has risks for everyone and it must stop thinking it should protect everyone by making their decisions for them and deciding what's good for them. Let the unique genius of humans make their own decisions and accept their own risks. Society, through the rule of law, must again make each person responsible for their own actions. Don't believe this hogwash the government is putting out that we must all learn to live with less. That kind of thinking will guarantee you will live with less. The masses may have to live with less if they work less, earn less and, therefore, deserve less, but if you let the American dream die…if you quit believing that greater efforts result in a greater living…we are all doomed to a socialistic society…doomed to a life of organized scarcity and a sharing of misery…equally. Remember, it was during the Depression that the great success stories of this nation were born. Many families that control much wealth today were spawned in those dark hours…people who didn't believe you had to settle for less, people who dug in and wrote their own story of success…dreamers…workers…winners.

As a nation, we have proven that wisdom does not necessarily come with more education – we have done many dumb things on our way to higher education – now, we need wisdom and a return to proven common sense values. Although, we have much work to do to preserve our free market system, great opportunities still abound. George S. Clason, author of "The Richest Man in Babylon" said, "Ahead of you stretches your future like a road leading into the distance. Along that road are ambitions you wish to achieve–desires you wish to gratify!!" Yes, you can become a millionaire!

## I DO NOT CHOOSE TO BE A COMMON MAN

It is my right to be uncommon…if I can.
I seek opportunity…not security.
I do not wish to be a kept citizen,
humbled and dulled by having the state look after me.
I want to take the calculated risk;
to dream and to build, to fail and to succeed.
I refuse to barter incentive for a dole.
I prefer the challenges of life to the guaranteed existence;
the thrill of fulfillment to the stale calm of utopia.
I will not trade freedom for beneficence
nor my dignity for a handout.
I will never cower before any master
nor bend to any threat.
It is my heritage to stand erect, proud and unafraid;
to think and act for myself; enjoy the benefits of my creations
and to face the world boldly and say, this I have done.
    -*Author Unknown*

# Yes! You Can Become A Millionaire

## SO, YOU WANT TO BE RICH!

I want to express some of my thoughts to you about why each of us are where we are today, and why I believe that we can be something much better tomorrow, and what I believe it will take to achieve a better tomorrow. Every one of us should dedicate and prepare ourselves in our endeavors to "Be A Winner" in our lives.

Being a winner means excelling – doing our very best – setting our sights high and reaching them and that should not be limited to athletes – that should not be limited to corporate presidents – that should not be limited to writers or directors, or lawyers, or doctors. It should not be and is not reserved for any person or groups of persons. These same things are available to you and can propel you to unbelievable heights in your career and living standards – and fortunately for us, life's method of rewarding dedicated winners is with position and riches. Life's methods of punishing those who fail, is with a hand-to-mouth existence and little chance to enjoy the many pleasures available in America.

First and foremost, you need to decide just how badly you want to be financially successful. This is critically important because it is an unquestionable fact that you can be financially independent if you are willing to do the things successful people do. After all, you are in America. You are free to do millions of legal things that can make you a fortune, by capitalizing on the freedom of opportunity that exists in America.

Highly successful people, at some point, come to the realization that they must do a lot of things that they may not enjoy doing, in order to be able to do the things they enjoy. For example, a barber who loves his job may not enjoy sweeping up the hair from the floor or cleaning his equipment.

A mother may not enjoy peeling potatoes but takes pride in her meals. She may not enjoy cleaning house but takes pride in a clean and orderly home. She may not enjoy putting on makeup or curling her hair but wants to look nice.

An athlete may not enjoy calisthenics but wants to win, a student may not enjoy homework but wants good grades. As a corporate chairman, there are some things about my job I don't like, but I do them. Most college coaches don't like recruiting, but they sure like winning.

No question about it, you can be financially independent, if you are willing to do the things successful people do.

In spite of the vast opportunities available through the free enterprise system, most Americans only pay lip service to wanting to do better, and opt instead to lie on the couch, watch hours and hours of TV for entertainment, play golf, softball, hunt, fish, etc., etc. and literally waste a thousand hours or more per year ignoring self improvement and wealth accumulation. God endowed you with the ability to gloriously provide for your family. Yes! You can become a millionaire!

The measure of a person is determined by what he does, not by what he says he will do or can do. So, it is vitally important that you decide just how badly you want to be wealthy. Some people prefer being a couch potato to being top banana. They would rather know all the statistics of their favorite sport teams, than the formula for success or how to achieve their own personal goals. They would rather criticize a coach's decisions than be the coach. There is a price to be paid for success but a much bigger price is extracted for failure. Some people want to turn their nose up at the thought of a career as a distributor with the Amway Corporation, but Dexter Yager of Charlotte, North Carolina and Hal Gooch, of Thomasville, North Carolina, didn't turn their noses up, instead they turned their dreams up and attitudes up, their hearts up and their commitments up. As a result, Mr. Yager's net worth today is beyond most people's imagination. God bless America and opportunity.

People like Dexter Yager and Hal Gooch are not interested in what the guitar looks like but how the music sounds. Dexter says he made a living between 9:00 to 5:00 and made his fortune between 5:00 and 9:00. At this time of the evening, most people are investing their time watching reality TV or one of hundreds of ball games. All people have the same number of minutes in a day, week, month or year, but successful people use more of their minutes achieving while average people waste them on entertainment. Success won't run you down, tap you on the shoulder and say "here I am." You have to run success down, tap it on the shoulder and say "no matter how fast you run from me, I'm going to catch you."

Remember – God endowed you with the ability to gloriously provide for your family. Yes! You can become a millionaire. It's not important how much net worth you have now, it's how much you can have. Why does it often take tragedy to make us see our abilities and our responsibilities? I think about the average person and it makes me wonder why healthy capable people will not perform without tragedy providing the push through necessity.

That reminds me of a story that occurred a few years back in Chicago. A man and his little seven-year-old daughter were standing on a street corner waiting for the light to change to cross the street. As the light changed the little seven-year-old Becky broke to run as children will sometimes do — a truck entering the intersection a little too late to stop, struck Becky just outside the outstretched hands of her terror-stricken father. When he reached her crumpled body — he knew instantly that she was seriously hurt. As the ambulance arrived and raced her to the emergency room with her father holding her hand – he could not help thinking about how beautiful and lively she was just a few minutes earlier and how quickly everything changed. As he anxiously waited in the emergency room for word of Becky's condition, Becky's mother arrived in tears. The doctor's advice was brief – on the side that Becky was struck, her leg would have to be amputated as well as her arm and one eye removed. I imagine each of you would react as Becky's father did – Becky's father cried out, "Oh my God, don't take her leg – take my leg, she's too young to lose a leg. Oh my God, don't take her arm, she's too young to lose an arm. My God, don't take her eye – take my eye."

I don't doubt that you would react the same way. You wouldn't hesitate to give your leg, your arm or an eye for your daughter – or your son – or your wife – and that's why it's hard to understand why the average person won't give eight hours a day of dedicated hard work to provide a better life for them while you have them healthy and happy.

The future is now. My desire is to see you in the coming year come to the full realization of what your abilities are. Recognize that with high ideals and worthy challenging goals, you can utilize discipline and dedication to achieve great success. Prepare yourself to travel life's road with the complete confidence that you're going to set higher and higher goals and achieve them.

We are all born with a brain but we develop our own attitude. Our attitude determines everything. It determines whether you will be happy or unhappy, positive or negative, committed to achievement or a ne'er-do-well, a positive benefit to humanity or a leach on society. In reality, your attitude is whatever you want it to be. The beauty of human beings is that you can change your attitude instantly. You don't have to study for it, you don't have to do manual labor, you don't have to plan it – you can just do it – instantly!

Another thing, you get to do it every day. Every morning when you get up, you decide what your attitude will be this new day. Some leave the house primed for road rage, others for the Horatio Alger front page. Remember this, it is not impossible to become highly successful with a negative attitude but it is highly improbable. Some people luck into riches in spite of everything but the vast majority who accumulate "wealth from nothing", are highly motivated and positive thinkers. A positive attitude is infectious, and not only strengthens your resolve and belief, but affects everyone around you and causes them to be more positive and desirous of helping you succeed.

A person with a positive attitude develops an army of helpers. The more helpers you have, the more certain your success. Just look at the achievements of ants and you'll know what the right attitude and teamwork can accomplish. Visualize yourself as the leader of an army of motivated, determined, committed, positive helpers. They are out there waiting for you to motivate them with your positive enthusiasm.

Mr. Rich DeVos and Jay Van Andel, co-founders of Amway, Sam Walton of Wal-Mart, Bill Gates of Microsoft, Michael Dell of Dell, Inc. and Mary Kay Ash of Mary Kay Cosmetics became fabulously wealthy and made thousands of others wealthy, with a positive mental attitude and by infecting others with positive thinking. There are literally thousands of wealthy successful men and women who started with nothing but a positive attitude, a strong belief system, enthusiasm and determination.

If you wish to achieve greatness in any field and the financial rewards that follow success, you need to embrace the twin trait of positive thinking – which is enthusiasm. Enthusiasm is a natural human trait and goes hand in hand with a positive attitude.

I grew up as one of nine children and have five of my own. I have also observed hundreds of other children, and one thing of which I am certain is that all humans are born with natural enthusiasm. Kids are enthusiastic about most everything. They get excited over the least little attention and respond with boundless enthusiasm over praise or play. Their little faces will light up a room at a moment's notice.

Unfortunately, after years of being told, "No, no, don't do that, go to your room, sit in the corner; or just wait 'til your Mom or Dad gets home," they gradually have their enthusiasm and positive attitude squeezed from them. When a positive attitude and enthusiasm leave, they are replaced with fear, suspicion, hatred, anger, sullenness or indifference; not exactly the best way to leave school seeking your fortune.

The good news is that childlike enthusiasm and a positive attitude can be called back to duty whenever you decide. Enthusiasm, like positive thinking, is infectious and has an effect on your customers, bankers, friends and associates. No one is unmoved by the enthusiasm of a man or woman on the road to success. The economic engines of the entire world don't have a reason to turn on until sales are made. Selling is the salvation of everyone. If you want to increase sales, turn up your enthusiasm. No matter what the product, enthusiasm will sell more of it than knowledge. Enthusiasm will sell when knowledge won't. Knowledge will make some sales where enthusiasm won't. But, if you really want to set new records, increase your knowledge and kick in the after burner on enthusiasm. God endowed you with the ability to gloriously provide for your family. Yes! You can become a millionaire.

Having money is better than not having money. Furthermore, the same things that will make you a financial success, will bring personal happiness to you, your spouse, and your children. A person who thinks positively and displays enthusiasm will influence all those around him/her to be the same. Even more important in personal relationships, an individual with these traits will be quick to make positive comments, praise, compliment and generally build up the feelings of individual value of people close to them. Nothing will strengthen the bonds between two people more than positive reinforcement and genuine praise. Nothing will cause another person to work at doing better more than the feeling that they are admired, appreciated and needed.

Most all of your life you have been led to believe that rich people are not happy people and/or that it's better to be happy than rich. This implies that you can't be happy and rich. This is one of the all time big lies. It is true that there are some rich people who are unhappy, but in all probability, those people would have been even more unhappy if they were poor. The difference would have been that they couldn't pay their bills, which would bring on yet more unhappiness. Based on my personal observation, the majority of unhappiness is caused by the lack of money and/or the lack of a foundation of religious belief. The real fact is that most successful people who earn what they have are very happy people. The simple reason is that they are enthusiastic, positive thinkers. Do not pursue happiness, pursue excellence and happiness will pursue you.

I have never known an unhappy enthusiastic positive thinker. That's not to say they do not have their sad moments. The sickness or death of a loved one hurts them just as much as anyone else. Setbacks are disappointing; a family member or friend on drugs or alcohol is heartrending but these are things that no one is immune from, regardless of one's net worth. But, one thing is certain, a positive person can and will endure them better than "Mr. Negative Ned." Successful people aren't whiners or excuse makers.

So, you want to be successful – you want to become a millionaire? Now I want you to answer the following questions from the bottom of your heart. Do you really believe you will be a major success? Do you want to learn how to be a success? Have you decided how badly you want these things? Have you decided how much you are willing to do to earn it? Have you decided how determined you are to achieve financial independence?

Don't read any further until you make these positive choices. If you still see yourself as a person hungry for fulfillment and financial independence, then read the Profile of a Winner and become one of us. Success is not a secret; it's a formula. God endowed you with the ability to gloriously provide for your family. Yes! You can become a millionaire.

> **There is no goal too great to seek,**
> **there is no mountain too high to climb,**
> **there is no depth too deep to explore,**
> **there is no job too tough to conquer,**
> **there is no wrong too wrong to forgive,**
> **there is no affliction too great for God to heal,**
> **there is no challenge that will go unchallenged,**
> **as long as there is freedom.**
>
> *- Wayne E. Ahart*

## PROFILE OF A WINNER

**GOAL DRIVEN**

I believe that when man's goals are good, God joins in! To start with, almost every great achievement since and including biblical times, has been the result of the relentless pursuit of a goal. A goal that is driven into the heart will cause ordinary people to achieve extra ordinary accomplishments. After all, what is it, other than a goal, that causes people to stay focused, never taking their eye off the target, persevering when all seems lost, plowing ahead when they feel like they are so deep in the well of despair that they would have to pump light in to see bottom? Did Moses have a goal? Did our early settlers heading west with "California or Bust" on their wagons have a goal? Did the Wright brothers have a goal? Did Henry Ford? Did President Kennedy acknowledge a goal for America's space program to land a man on the moon? Desire creates goals, goals increase desire.

If you want to achieve greatness, establish your goal. Without a goal, how do you know when you get there? You will find that you will constantly be setting your goals higher and higher as you achieve more and more. Goals make you stretch. Goal setting makes you reach up - up - up, stretch more - more - more, as you realize there is no limit. The higher you reach, the higher you climb, the farther you can then see. When you see a new horizon, you can climb more. Humans don't want to climb higher than they can see and goals help you see further.

## COURAGE

A major goal is never easy to achieve, but, there is no point in having such a goal, if you are not willing to lay it all on the line – burn the bridge behind you – cut off all avenues of escape, whereby success is the only route remaining. It takes great courage to risk it all, but great achievement generally demands it.

When you **have** to do something, the odds are unbelievable that you will. A good illustration of that power was in the movie, "The Dirty Dozen." Lee Marvin was drilling his men on rope climbing and one particular man had climbed to within 6' or 8' of the top and could go no further. He cried and pleaded that it was impossible for him to go further and the shouts and orders of Lee Marvin were to no avail… Lee Marvin then took a machine gun and shot the rope off just below his feet… In a matter of seconds, he was on the platform at the top. You see Lee Marvin cut off all avenues of escape… He had to do it… and with this new motivation he easily did what was impossible a moment earlier.

Winners are willing to take risks; in fact, most of them at one time or another risked almost everything to accomplish their goal. However, winners face risks pragmatically. They take risks when absolutely necessary but do everything they can to avoid risk when possible. Remember, their goal is to win and unnecessary risks are never prudent. A winner's "risk taking" is not like a roll of the dice. When taking a necessary risk, they approach it with significant caution and planning to reduce the level of risk as much as possible. Always stack the deck in your favor as much as possible when taking risks. Risk avoidance is as much a part of "the Winner", as risk taking. They do whatever is called for at the time.

**CONFIDENCE IN THEIR ABILITY**

One of the biggest causes for the lack of success by individuals in America is the lack of self-confidence. People who do not believe in themselves do not challenge themselves to higher performance. They do not risk failure because they doubt their ability. They worry that they're not good enough, not smart enough and not deserving enough to attain great success. But, a few disappointments on the road to ultimate success makes winning a little sweeter.

If you have small expectations, you will always attain them. If you have big expectations, you will be amazed how often you will attain them, as well. Even when you don't, you generally will get close, which is far better than achieving a small goal.

Most of us are where we are today because we have succeeded. If you are happy and proud of your accomplishments, proud of the lifestyle you have achieved for your family, it is because you have set your goals high enough and committed to their achievements. On the other hand, if you are not happy and proud of the lifestyle you have provided your family, it is also the result of success.

You have succeeded in keeping your goals low enough that you would always be virtually assured you would reach them.

Therefore, if you have reached your goals, you have succeeded.

Many people have proven that you can be miserable in victory when the victory is insignificant. Low goals are the result of low self-confidence.

In biblical times, Solomon was a man of supreme confidence. He had 300 wives and 700 concubines. My son, Doug Ahart, believes that Solomon is the one who inspired the term "batting a thousand."

In reality, too many people have been taught not to expect much of themselves, but supreme confidence is a trademark of all winners. Average people frequently interpret such confidence as arrogance or egotism, however, true winners believe in their knowledge, preparation and commitment so completely that the final outcome is never in doubt in their mind. One should never gear down confidence to please the average people around him. It is far better to achieve great success and be misunderstood than to be appreciated by the masses for being like them and stuck in mediocrity. However, truly great winners develop a humbleness with their confident attitude.

They believe unflinchingly that they can get the job done regardless of economic conditions or outside events. Winners believe in themselves. Their confidence is the result of careful preparation and planning. They know that the person who wins the most is the one who is the most prepared. Real winners never set a goal or start a project that they don't fervently believe they can achieve. Man was not born with the ability to fly, so he made something to fly him – man couldn't breathe under water, so he made something that would breath for him. He couldn't travel far under or over water, so he made boats – ships and submarines. God made the rain, man made umbrellas. God made the winter, man made coats. Is there anything you cannot do?

**POSITIVE ATTITUDE**

I believe that a positive mental attitude is the greatest single reason for most successful endeavors. In fact, without a positive attitude, very few dramatic goals would ever be thought of, much less attempted. A positive attitude walks arm in arm with optimism. Optimism is not seeing the world through rose-colored glasses but believing you can make the world rose colored. It is difficult to achieve anything significant without optimism and a positive attitude. People generally enjoy being in the company of positive-minded people and prefer to avoid the presence of negative thinkers.

Negative thinking, which destroys most ideas and goals, is completely foreign to "the Winner." They approach all facets of life positively and are constantly reinforcing their positive attitude and winning spirit by reading upbeat educational materials.

A positive attitude is the Winner's greatest weapon against disappointment or setbacks. Winners know instinctively that a positive attitude brings positive results and influences their customers and associates to act accordingly. We can expand our horizons by our thoughts. Great achievements always surprise many people, mostly mothers, but seldom surprise the achiever – they are consumed with the firm belief they will succeed.

There is one word to guide one's life. One word, if religiously practiced, is all you will ever need to enjoy life – guarantee your stability, consistency, purpose and ultimate success. One word will take the place of essays – books – commandments – pleadings – laws.

The word is "positive." One whose heart, soul and mind is

"positive" is blessed in all conceivable ways.

A positive mind never considers a negative deed. None of the Ten Commandments would or could be violated by a positive thought process. None of the laws of the land would be broken; bad luck or hard times would be no match for the positive person. Hardship or natural disaster may be heartbreaking but cannot be spirit breaking to the strong positive being. There is nothing known to man that can defeat a positive thought. One who is positive, is always looking forward – expecting good things – planning – working – helping, is happy – enthusiastic. All the good things described in the dictionary – encyclopedia – thesaurus are achieved by positivity.

Of all these things – I am "positive!" A positive mind needs no doctrines, code of ethics or credos.

## I CAN DO IT!

One of the most potent influences on you becoming successful is a completely positive belief that you will. It doesn't matter what you are trying to succeed at – sports, academics, business, or family development, total confidence in your ability to succeed is the single most powerful determinant. The "Little Train That Could" was packed full of truth and human traits with the chant, "I think I can, I think I can." Believe me, if you think you can – you can and will!

## VISUALIZATION

I believe that great achievers have the ability to mentally see themselves as victors well before the contest begins. They are actually capable "through imagination" to picture themselves doing that which they desire. This is true of the successful athlete, student, cheerleader, corporation executive, merchant, doctor, lawyer, and politician. They see themselves succeeding and performing long before it's an actuality.

Jim Brown, the all-time great running back for the Cleveland Browns was asked one time, after one of his great games in which he rushed for 235 yards, how he got himself "up" for the game. Jim said that before the game started, he would do a little imagination dreaming… He would actually imagine and see himself playing his position…see himself taking the handoff, darting through the line and breaking to the outside. He could actually see himself taking a pitchout and mentally go through each tackle as he eluded one tackler after another for a long gainer. He could see himself blocking when he was used as a decoy. In essence, he was imagining himself succeeding and having a mental picture of himself doing it.

After Gene Tunney knocked out Jack Dempsey with that fantastic left hook of his, a reporter commented, "That was the most perfect left hook I have ever seen, perfectly placed and perfectly timed. How did you do it?" Gene Tunney calmly remarked that it wasn't so fantastic to him. He said, "I had already done it 10,000 times before in my imagination."

A large part of succeeding is seeing yourself through imagination doing those things you so desire to do. Unfortunately, imagination also works in reverse, and far too many people flash negative failure-oriented pictures across their minds. They are expecting failure, imagining failure and in most cases are rewarded with it.

Emerson wrote that man becomes what he thinks about all day long. This may not always be right, but I believe it is extremely close to being right. I believe that man does tend to become what he thinks about and transfers his thinking into vivid mental pictures through imagination.

A high percentage of individual achievers mentally visualized themselves doing what needs to be done to succeed. They visualized themselves enjoying the fruits of victory, i.e. driving Cadillacs and Lincolns, owning the best of homes and enjoying the best of the good life.

The Winner constantly visualizes through mental images an already successfully completed task. He/she sees the end result before the act begins and as it proceeds.

A famous potter once told me that the average person sees a lump of clay when he views a lump of clay, but a potter sees what the lump of clay can become. Most great athletes see themselves winning before the event. Great farmers see their crops growing in the fields even before planting and great surgeons visualize every detail before surgery.

You must learn to see yourself like a potter sees a lump of clay; not what you are today but what you can become tomorrow. Man only uses approximately 10% of his brain. What miracles and wonders could occur if you increased that by a mere 2% or 3%?

**AWARE OF TIME VALUE**

Winners are always in a hurry and waste very little time on trivial matters. They recognize there is very little difference in people except the way they utilize their time and the way they think.

Time, to a Winner, is a commodity and must be invested for a return. How many people do you think wish they had watched more TV or gone to more sporting events or played more golf when they discover they have reached retirement age with no income? How many people at the moment of death, will look back and wish they had watched more movies, climbed more mountains, killed more deer or went to more wild drinking parties? Does this mean that one shouldn't ever relax, hunt, participate in sports or be socially active? No, in fact you need to relax and enjoy yourself. The key is to not allow these things to dominate your time and thinking. Don't live for golf, hunting, football statistics, etc. Recognize these things as only recreation, not a dominant thought process that keeps your mind and heart from focusing on goal achievement. If you wish to be a Winner, you must realize that time flies, but it never lands – it never stops. Time is an asset to be invested, not wasted. Average people waste their time on trivial matters.

True Winners develop a greater appreciation for the value of time and their use of it. Discussing the value of time reminds me of a true story that occurred during the Korean War. The dark of night had found a large number of United States Marines faced with a fight for their lives. They were camped for the night not far from an enemy camp that outnumbered them 5 to 1. Both sides knew that battle was unavoidable and a fight to the death would begin with the light of day. It was bone chilling cold at 30 degrees below zero and the American Marines were attempting to make the night as comfortable as possible. A war correspondent, noticing a Marine standing alone next to a tank, took a good look at this veteran of many long months of loneliness and battles. The correspondent noticed that the steel on the tank was so cold that his finger tips stuck to the metal when touched.

The correspondent wanted to ask the Marine a philosophical

question. As the Marine stood there staring into the night, with icicles forming on his growth of beard, the correspondent asked him, "Soldier, if I were God and could grant you anything you wished, what would you want at this hour?" The soldier hesitated for a long moment giving thought to this question. Then he startled his questioner with this reply, "I would want you to guarantee me tomorrow."

How precious time was to this soldier when it appeared that "tomorrow" would be denied him. Now here we are with every reason to believe that hundreds and thousands of tomorrows will be ours. Most of us do not appreciate time as we should, and taking it for granted do not utilize our time to the best of our abilities. If we did, we would be a greater influence on the affairs of man and care for our loved ones with greater certainty and abundance.

**SINGLE MINDED**

Generally speaking, the Winner is totally consumed with the achievement and improvement of his goal. Almost every hour of the Winner's days and nights, his mind is constantly thinking about his goals and how to achieve them.

The modern day word is "focus". Winners are totally focused on goal achievement. Before the days of tractors, farmers plowed with mules or horses. They discovered that these animals were not as committed to the task of plowing when they could see things going on around them. Someone designed a bridle with leather blinders on each side to deny them peripheral vision and keep their sight focused straight ahead. Winners have mental blinders and do not allow themselves to become distracted by all the outside activities and entertainment going on around them.

## COMMITTED

The Winner is totally and completely committed to do whatever it takes – make any sacrifice – perform any task to achieve his/her goal.

One of the greatest talents given to man is the ability to totally commit himself to a task. You cannot beat a determined person, and determination is created by commitment. When Lewis straddled the small stream flowing from a spring which he deemed to be the beginning of the Missouri river during the Lewis and Clark expedition, he stated the following: "I have attained one of my goals with which my mind has been unalterably fixed upon." "Unalterably fixed," were his words to describe his total commitment. He refused to allow his mind to be diverted from his goals.

Glen Cunningham as a young boy in Kansas was the victim of a gasoline explosion in his home. He was burned so badly that he was told he would never walk again. Glen Cunningham refused to accept this sentence and totally committed himself to rebuild his muscles to not only walk, but to run. What others thought was foolish, Glen thought possible. History now records Glen Cunningham's commitment in the Olympic record books. He became the world's fastest human, winning Olympic gold medals for his country.

Total commitment works wonders that the world's foremost experts cannot explain. On December 8, 1995, Jean-Dominique Bauby, at the age of 43, editor in chief of Elle Magazine in Paris, France, suffered a massive stroke. When he regained consciousness three weeks later, he could only move his left eyelid. Did you comprehend what you just read? He could only move his left eyelid. Yet in this horrible condition, his indomitable human spirit, courage and ability to commit to a task, rose to the top. He wrote the best seller "The Diving Bell and the Butterfly" to inform the world about his condition and the thoughts he was thinking. Mr. Bauby wrote this book in a manner you and I cannot even fathom. To create each word, he had an assistant go through the alphabet until she reached each letter in the word he wanted to use. When she reached this letter he would blink his eye. Then she would repeat the process until she reached the next letter. He wrote a whole book doing this. Talk about commitment! There is nothing you cannot do if you are totally, uncompromisingly committed. There is little you can do if you are not! I recommend his book.

**HARD WORKER**

Most people want to know how to succeed, but they stop listening when they hear – hard work. Without exception, every Winner works very hard to achieve his/her goal. They understand that success comes when you make it happen – not by waiting or hoping that it will happen. They are usually performing earlier and later than the average person and enjoying it more – work is play to the Winner.

No matter what the task, the person who works the smartest usually succeeds the most. Most Winners realize the harder they work, the smarter and luckier they get. One of my good friends said, "Luck occurs when preparation and opportunity meet." Some people have the knack of giving you an entire "lesson of life" in just a few words. You could write two chapters and not say any more than "Luck occurs when preparation and opportunity meet." These few brilliant words were uttered by the legendary, Hall of Fame coach, Darrell Royal. This lesson in life ranks up there with "It all depends on whose bull's getting gored" by Sam Rayburn, "There ain't no such thing as a free lunch" (unknown) and "nobody has ever built a monument to a critic" (unknown).

Each of these short statements carry a dramatic lesson of life. "The harder I work, the luckier I get," is another lesson in life. Most Winners know instinctively that whatever their vocation, they can compete and win by outworking their competitors. Therefore, writing a significant volume about being a hard worker would be a waste of time and energy. Basic common sense will tell you that you need to work hard to achieve a goal. If you are not fully prepared to do that, then you are wasting your time reading this book. If you're going to wait for "good luck" to improve your life – bring lunch. You'll have a long wait. If you truly want to become successful in any field of endeavor and become financially independent, you should be chomping at the bit to get started every day. When I first started as a 22-year-old insurance agent in 1962, most thought I was too young and inexperienced. My answer to their criticism; I'll just have to outwork everyone else. And I did!

**WON'T QUIT**

Most Winners have tasted defeat many times and failed on many projects – but – true Winners never quit – never give up. What would seem total disaster and final failure to the average person is but a temporary setback – a bump in the road – a learning experience that will help them ultimately achieve and win. They keenly understand – you cannot beat one who will not quit. Zig Ziglar in his speeches tell us that "Tornadoes and Hurricanes make more noise, but Termites do more damage."

You see, storms can be devastating in a short period of time but termites just never quit, they never give up. Each of us has numerous events occur in our lifetime that present us with critical choices. Often, the choice we make determines whether we fold our tent or go on to build a mansion. One such story is about a young new life insurance agent, Mr. James Dunham of Antlers, Oklahoma. James had just completed his sales training class and a few days of "in-field" training. James had a lead on one of the most successful businessmen in town. James decided to call on him at his residence around 6:00 PM. The prospect lived in what looked like a mansion to James with a big circle drive.

James began to doubt whether a young man like himself, driving an older car, should be calling on such an influential person. He drove around and around trying to get up the nerve to call on him. He pulled in the circle drive two or three times without stopping. He parked on the side of the road talking himself into and out of calling on him. Finally, he decided that if he was going to succeed in the business, he must muster the courage to make calls on successful people, such as this person. By this time, it was nearly 10:00 PM and when he parked in the circle drive, all the lights had been turned off. James was now determined and committed to make this call. When he rang the doorbell, the lights came on and the prospect came to the door in his pajamas. James made an enthusiastic introduction and approach and the successful businessman said, "Anyone out working this late, I have to talk to," and invited him in. Nearly 1½ hours later, the man awakened his wife to sign the application on two contracts.

I believe this one event established James in the business and would have spelled failure for him had he not had the courage to make this call. James Dunham was like a termite. James went on to become founder and chairman of his own insurance company. It's little choices like this that often determine whether we eat steak in life or beans and cornbread. Both are filling and nutritional but one is a food of choice and the other a food of necessity.

When you look back at world history, you will find thousands of examples of people who have improved our lifestyle immeasurably because they refused to quit. Orville and Wilbur Wright, Alexander Graham Bell, Henry Ford, Dr. Jonas Salk and Alexander Fleming are just a few, but can you imagine a world today without airplanes, telephones, cars and trucks, uncontrolled polio, and what would our world be like without penicillin? Someone will eventually cure cancer and AIDS because that someone won't quit. GOD BLESS PEOPLE WHO WON'T QUIT!!!

Abraham Lincoln failed over and over and over until he became our greatest president in our greatest hour of need. Jesus died on the cross for his belief and accepted a painful and torturous death instead of quitting his mission. Are you willing to sacrifice to achieve your mission? Many capable people refuse to give up their sports, entertainment and their "couch and beer time" for success. Is it any wonder they remain mired in mediocrity? Losers motto – "If at first you don't succeed, why try again?"

**WELL EDUCATED**

While most Winners enjoy the benefit of a quality, formal education from respected universities, many great achievers and true Winners had very little formal education. But, they were well educated, just the same! They are self-educated, voracious readers who never cease educating themselves.

No one understands the value of education more than one who does not possess it formally or traditionally. Winners continue to study and improve their knowledge of their own business but also acquire general knowledge; particularly in national and world events. It is not relevant how much education you have now; it's how much education you can acquire in the future that is important. I cannot over emphasize the importance of education.

Just as the fastest person will win most races, the strongest will win most weight lifting contests. The best educated, if positive and motivated, will win in most competitive business ventures. The point is, regardless of your formal education, keep reading and studying to improve your knowledge. And, don't ever use a lack of education as an excuse to remain mediocre.

I could fill an entire book with nothing but names of people and the companies they started, with educations ranging from high school dropouts to 1 or 2 years of college. Formal education is important and the more you have the bigger your advantage, but your most important education comes after you get out of school. Successful achievers, such as salespeople, teachers, entrepreneurs, computer specialists, bankers, doctors, lawyers, politicians, preachers, hunters, fishermen and golfers are not born, they are trained.

You can be trained to be anything you want, but remember this, the swiftness with which people are trainable varies from person to person. The fact that you can learn specialized skills is a scientifically proven fact. The speed of learning for you is unknown and in some instances may require total commitment, determination and patience. Speaking from personal experience, I have learned many skills with little effort or time required. However, many things I have learned were extremely challenging and really tested my resolve to learn.

Except for those who inherit wealth, people are not born financially successful. They evolve from inspiration, perspiration, determination, education and a burning desire.

My own Mom and Dad were sharecroppers. Obviously, neither they nor their children enjoyed any of the advantages that naturally come with affluence. However, we still enjoyed advantages. We were blessed with good health, we learned the value of work, to respect the rights of others, to believe in God, and to trust in ourselves. Our greatest advantage was that we were lucky enough to be born in the United States of America. Ninety five percent of all the people on earth would almost kill for those advantages. In America, every day is your "lucky day," if you don't screw it up.

*The writer of this book started with no assets, a 9th grade education and yet has made millions and many others have made millions by their association with him. You can too! You can make millions if you want to badly enough and are willing to do what is known to work.*

**QUALITY ASSOCIATES**

The Winner surrounds himself professionally and personally with top quality people whom he/she can lean on, grow with and enjoy life with. The Winner realizes that good people create good results and good life styles.

What type of people do you think Tom Landry surrounded himself with? What about Sam Walton or Bill Gates? Do you think Paul Harvey or Zig Ziglar would be associated with just anybody? If you want to assure your success, do as these people have done and surround yourself with the cream of society. That doesn't mean you must associate with known leaders or celebrities, but you must seek people like yourself who are solid, honest and positive.

**SUCCEEDING VIA GROUP BRAIN TRUST**

If a group of men or women or a combination thereof, come together for the specific purpose of achieving a single goal or solving a problem, the creative brainpower of the group meshed together will multiply ten-fold over the brainpower of each member individually. The creative energy or brainwaves will transfer and be received from one to the other and bring forth ideas of superior intellect. The key is for each group member to be totally committed to giving his/her all in seeking success and remove all but positive thoughts and belief that the answers will come if they are persistent.

The human brain is a magnificent thing and will produce an unlimited supply of ideas when cultivated. The brain is similar to the process of farming or gardening. One plows up and disturbs the soil, breaks up the hardened clogs, plants a seed, fertilizes the soil and feeds it with water and sunshine. Nothing short of a miracle occurs when mother earth produces the plant you chose.

Likewise, your brain will produce the ideas and plans you are seeking when you cultivate it, plow it up, disturb it, plant a seed, give it orders to harvest ideas to achieve a certain goal, fertilize it with meditation and concentration, feed it with reading and diligent study and water it by sharing and discussion with others in the group to cause cross-pollination. In time, a harvest of answers spring forth that when acted upon will achieve the stated goal.

However, mother earth if left alone will produce any number of unknown species of plants, grasses or trees, including the dreaded weed. In the arid areas of the world, little or no vegetation grows as if earth is asleep.

Again, the brain is similar. If left alone, undisturbed, unchallenged, the brain will assume a posture of being asleep. It will do no more than operate your body as if on cruise control. Weeds (negative thoughts) begin to grow and choke off the air supply of productive thought.

The real work of a brain, "cultivation of ideas, plans and formulas," will not activate in an arid soil. The brain is a team player and you are the captain. Get your brain involved in creating miracles and working with other motivated brains to compete and win in the game of life.

**HONEST**

True Winners are honest to the bone. They understand that gains made through manipulation, intimidation or shady actions are short term and unfulfilling. Long term success and feelings of accomplishment come through honest dealings. They compete hard but they play by the rules. The fairness rule is their guiding light and their motto is "Do what's right." No measure of accomplishment is worth sacrificing one's integrity. True Winners understand this and feel it deep within.

You have just read 13 attributes that make Winners of average people.

The benefits of leading a successful, committed, goal-driven life are enormous. The rewards include an improved emotional, mental, physical and financial state.

When you begin to understand and live the 13 principles in "The Profile of a Winner" you will begin to experience a change of attitude, with an increased level of confidence and enthusiasm for the future. You will begin to expect good things to happen to you and will work to make them happen. You will suddenly realize you are a Winner and acquire a Winner's confidence.

Winners are relaxed and control their surroundings no matter how chaotic it seems to others. Winners have no fear of others or situations because they're always prepared. They work in relaxed harmony with others due to their supreme confidence and the knowledge that they only operate from a base of honesty and integrity. As a result of these attributes they enjoy high respect among their peers.

You have no reason to fear anybody or anything when you are prepared, knowledgeable, honest and dedicated.

Once again, these 13 keys are:

1. Goal Driven
2. Courage
3. Confidence in their ability
4. Positive attitude
5. Visualization
6. Aware of time value

7. Single minded
8. Committed
9. Hard Worker
10. Won't Quit
11. Well Educated
12. Quality Associates
13. Honesty

If you wanted to drive from Pittsburgh to Los Angeles, it would be foolish to do it without a road map. I'm sure you would eventually get there after many mistakes and wrong roads. You would pay for your foolishness in numerous ways. Many people go through life hoping for success in the same manner. On the other hand, you could sit in Pittsburgh studying a map and you would never see Los Angeles. Just planning won't get you there, you have to actually drive the roads. If you want to go to Los Angeles, you study the map, plan your route and get going.

If you wish to be a Winner in life you must do the same. The profile of a Winner is your map. Study it, plan your route and get going.

**FOLLOW THE PATH**

Follow the path. Blazing new trails is a waste of energy, time and intelligent thinking. The only time it is intelligent to blaze new trails is when inventing or seeking a better system with new technology. Otherwise, follow the path of least resistance beaten down by the feet of generations of winners before you. Even animals are smart enough to follow the trails of many before them. Trails that lead to water, food and shelter. Successful men and women have traveled the road to success many times before you, they have cleared the path and have left a clear blueprint to success. Only the foolish insist on making all those same mistakes over again. Would you deem it admirable or intelligent to insist on discovering fire again or inventing the wheel again? Learn from those who succeeded before you and follow the path. Accept the discoveries of others before you and succeed by utilizing proven methods. As you pick your way through the trails of success, marked by generations of successful men and women, keep a sharp eye for any potential to make an improvement along the success trail. Each new success improves and widens the trail for others. If you are the adventuresome type and prefer to blaze a completely new trail, you may or may not succeed, but what wisdom is there in ignoring the knowledge of past generations? Thank God, children have parents and teachers to emulate and walk in their footsteps of experience. Thank God, you have paths to follow and heroes to emulate for success. Follow the path!

Every path leads through storms, but the path will still be there after the storm has passed.

## Yes, You Can Make A Million Working For Someone Else!

Every corporation is made up of individuals, individuals with varying degrees of experience, training, education, knowledge, and ability. There are many talented individuals in most corporations. But, these individuals are not nearly as effective by themselves as they are when they join hands with other individuals to work toward a common objective. Napoleon Hill, a man who spent 20 years of his life studying the lives of successful men and has written several popular books about how to be successful, calls this concept the "master mind alliance." To express this concept simply, it means that our minds expand and grow as we share ideas with others who are applying their minds toward a common objective. Working together toward a common objective is one of the secrets of success that Mr. Hill has discovered. When you finish this book, go buy

"Think and Grow Rich" by Napoleon Hill.

In essence, what I am saying is that the sum of the parts does not equal the whole; the whole is more than the sum of its parts. The corporation can accomplish much more together as a group than the sum of what the individuals can accomplish by themselves.

To illustrate, let me tell you about a local contest held in Canada. The contest was to see whose horse could pull the most weight. The local residents were very excited about the contest and were vigorously bragging and betting on their horses up until the day of the contest. The big day finally arrived and the winning horse won by pulling a load of a little more than 9,000 pounds. The horse that finished second pulled just under 9,000 pounds.

The local residents then began speculating as to how much weight these two horses could pull together. Most of the betters estimated that the horses would pull anywhere from 18 to 20 thousand pounds. When all of the bets were in, the two horses were lined up side by side and were harnessed to the sled. They began pulling and when the local citizens finally quit adding weight to the sled, the two horses, working together, did not pull 18,000 pounds as most people had expected, but pulled over 30,000 pounds. The sum of the parts did not equal the whole.

Another good example of this concept is found in the flight of Canadian geese. A flock of Canadian geese fly in a "V" formation. If you watch them you see that every so often there is some confusion in the formation. This confusion comes about because the geese are changing leaders. Scientists have discovered that the lead goose breaks the wind for the geese to the right and to the left of him. These geese in turn break the wind for the geese behind them so that a flock of geese can fly 72%

further than an individual goose. Again, the sum of the parts does not equal the whole. The team is much more effective than the individual.

Watch two kids walking on a railroad track side by side. One walks a few steps very shakily and falls, the other walks a few steps and falls. But, when they join hands across the tracks they can walk forever.

Many people have the mistaken idea that they must be in business for themselves, be an entrepreneur, invent a new product or develop a new concept, to become a millionaire. A large number of new millionaires over the last twenty years were employed by successful corporations. Thousands of new millionaires are employees or distributors of companies like Wal-Mart, Amway, Microsoft, Dell Inc., Freeport McMoRan Inc., Mary Kay Cosmetics and thousands of other corporations similar to these. However, corporate size is not necessarily the determining factor; thousands of new millionaires come from smaller companies, some which you have never heard of.

How did they do it? How do you make a million working for someone else? First, you must be a dedicated, committed, enthusiastic employee. If you think of your work as work, your success will be limited and your happiness denied. You must understand that your company is number one – more important than anything else, except your God and family. You must work for your employers as if their success depends solely upon you. Passion for your employer's success will guarantee yours. Average people go to work each day wondering what might happen, but real winners go to work to make things happen.

Second, you must realize that in your performance on and off the job, if you live and utilize the principles outlined in this book, you will stand head and shoulders above most other employees. This will bring about promotions, more income and more opportunity.

Third, invest in the company you are working for by purchasing stock and negotiate stock options and/or profit-sharing. Most of the millionaires who work for Dell Inc. or Wal-Mart have achieved their lofty financial status through stock purchase programs and stock options. Help build the company you are working for and become an owner. Owners are excited about waking up each day and contributing to their company's growth. Average people dread a new workday and mostly look forward to quitting time and Friday. It says a lot about a person whose greatest interest is in "quitting."

What company wouldn't wrap their arms around an employee who works for the company as if it were his/her own? What company wouldn't give almost anything for an employee/owner who works hard, thinks positive, inspires other employees, has goals, is totally honest and determined to succeed. The answer, every company!

Therefore, don't discount the opportunity to make a fortune right where you are. Go to your managers and challenge them to let you in on the action, through stock or profit-sharing, if you perform at certain levels.

Don't forget the tree in your back yard, when looking for the forest. The most important area to develop for success and happiness is between your ears.

Don't forget what Dexter Yager and Hal Gooch did through Amway — there are many other Amway distributor millionaires. Don't forget all the other companies that offer franchise opportunities for little investment but big potential. Don't forget the vast opportunities still available in insurance, real estate and investments. Above all else remember this, "you don't need an earth-shattering idea, you need earth-shattering performance and service."

True winners realize that planning and preparation is a key to victory. Lawyers and accountants know that the winner is nearly always the best prepared. They do their homework. Professional sales people know their product inside and out and practice their presentations daily. How do you think a great chef gets to be one? Trial and error, creative thinking, planning and practice, practice, practice. Most people's greatest fear is public speaking. Some people's greatest joy is public speaking. What's the difference? Preparation and practice. Nothing will give you confidence like preparation and practice. Most great speakers have spent many hours in front of the mirror practicing in order to make society's greatest fear their own greatest joy! Few things are more satisfying than knowing you just made a great speech or sang a great song. Singing is speechmaking put to music.

When I was a boy growing up in Arkansas, we raised our own chickens for eggs and meat. Every Sunday we killed two chickens for Sunday dinner. Our chickens caught onto the routine and on Saturday you would see the chickens doing calisthenics and running wind sprints. They knew that the two slowest would be swimming in gravy on Sunday.

I'm reminded of the two dogs arguing over who was the fastest and the better rabbit catcher. One wagered a bet that he could catch any rabbit. Roaming the fields, he finally jumped up a nervous rabbit and the race was on. The rabbit was the victor and the exhausted dog was explaining why he lost. He said, "You must understand that the rabbit was running for his life and I was only running for lunch." Good point. If you wish to succeed, you must plan, prepare, practice and run for your life.

## IS 99.9% GOOD ENOUGH?

The next time something requires 100%, and you figure that 99.9% is good enough, think of this:

In the United States, 99.9% quality would mean:
- One hour of unsafe drinking water per month
- Two unsafe landings at O'Hare every day
- 16,000 lost pieces of mail per hour
- 20,000 incorrect drug prescriptions each year
- 500 incorrect surgical operations performed each week
- 50 newborn babies dropped at birth by doctors each day
- 22,000 checks deducted from the wrong accounts each hour
- Your heart fails to beat 32,000 times each year

If the rabbit required 100% effort to elude the chasing dog and gave only 99.9%, well you can see the result.

## The Rich Get Richer And The Poor Get Poorer Is Mostly True!

Why? The answer is simple… the actions of each, the habits, the thinking process, the goals or lack of goals, the commitment to continuing education, the level of motivation and the degree of determination never change. Therefore, their station in life will quite naturally follow the same patterns that got them where they are. However, if you reversed the order and the poor people began to act and think like the rich and the rich began to act and think like the poor – then their stations in life would switch. The best thing you can do for the poor is to not join their ranks. Many years ago, someone said, "if you give a hungry man a fish, all you do is satisfy his hunger, but if you teach him how to fish, he can feed himself forever." Obviously, this is true. But the fallacy is that most hungry people who wanted to feed themselves, would have already sought out the knowledge to do so. It takes action to feed yourself and to achieve greatness.

No amount of knowledge, planning or good intentions will bring success without action. You must put your plans and goals on the playing field where the wars are fought. What good is it to own the best book ever written if you don't read it? What good is it if you own the best cake ever baked if you don't eat it? What good is it if you have the best song that's ever been written if it's never sung? Success comes by doing – not wishing or hoping. The measure of men/women is determined by what they do not by what they say they'll do. Put your plans into action – go to work with a degree of determination as if the outcome was life or death to you.

What good is it if you have the best idea in the history of man if you never put it into action? Put your plan to work with confidence. The attitude of expecting success affects everyone and increases your own determination and enthusiasm.

You were not born a defeatist – negativist, hateful, spiteful, jealous, angry, or mean. You learned these things. In essence, you were taught them by your family, friends and general environment. But, if you can learn those things, you can also learn trust, positive thinking, love, kindness, control and victory. You were not born with habits – you learned them and you can change them. To get richer, get better! Everyone who feels that life hasn't been fair or that luck has gone against them wants a second chance. A second chance doesn't help if you keep the first attitude. You don't get prime rib from a chicken.

## Faith In Yourself

The successful achievement of any goal is almost assured when you have complete faith in yourself. The Bible teaches that faith the size of a mustard seed can move mountains. If faith can move mountains, it can abundantly provide food, shelter and security for your family. Faith in yourself and faith in your spouse will greatly enhance your happiness and fulfillment.

You should start no journey without the faith that you can complete it and any desire to do better or be better should be accompanied by faith in yourself.

## Are You "Too Good" To Become A Millionaire?

How much is your ego worth?

Are you more interested in becoming financially independent or having a high sounding title which you believe elevates your prestige?

Would you rather be a wealthy Amway distributor or a doctor or lawyer who made only an average income?

Would you rather be a millionaire in the trash hauling business or a $40,000 per year investment banker?

Would you rather say "I'm in banking" and barely make an average pay or say "I'm a millionaire hog farmer?"

Prestige in a title is fleeting but the prestige earned by performance in an honest endeavor is everlasting. There is an old saying that nothing succeeds like success.

In examining any opportunity, always base your analysis on the overall potential, not on whether it massages your ego.

You cannot feed your family, buy a home or cruise the world on high sounding titles. There is no greater prestige than the respect you gain in the knowledge you are a winner.

## You Can Make History

Some people read about history, others only hear about it, but you and I have the privilege of making it happen – or – just go along for the ride wherever history takes us.

When you start from nothing and create wealth and value, you are making history. You have the talent and the opportunity to take your heart and mind and change the course of history where you and your family are concerned. This is not an opportunity to be taken lightly, it's an awesome privilege and responsibility. Destiny doesn't tap you on the shoulder and say, "Aren't you lucky?" But, you can tap destiny on the shoulder and say, "I'm here to change history and claim my right to all that I choose."

Create your own destiny – don't wait for destiny to create you! Regardless of your field of endeavor, ten years from today, people in your industry should look around and say, "Where did that guy come from?" Don't you suppose those words were uttered by Sears about Sam Walton; by IBM about Ross Perot, Bill Gates and Michael Dell; by American Airlines about Herb Kelleher; by numerous retailers about Rich DeVos and Jay Van Andel? All of these people had a rare opportunity and attacked it with faith and confidence. You have the same opportunity, if you just recognize it.

Controlling your own destiny is to determine beforehand an inevitable outcome. That's your job!

Opportunity is the same for all of us, regardless of race, creed or national origin. America affords us all the same opportunity. We don't all start from the same start line, but the finish line is the same. Many people have to work harder, longer, smarter and sacrifice more due to where they came from and where they are, but the opportunity is there just the same. If you doubt these statements, I ask you to look around and take note of the many successful immigrants in our country. You will find in every community very successful immigrants, from India, Pakistan,

Vietnam, Korea, China, Germany, Mexico, countries from all over the world. Many of these people came to our country unable to speak English. In spite of this handicap, within 10 - 15 - 20 years, they become an American success story.

Why? The reason is simple. They are so thrilled for the chance to come to America — the beacon of freedom throughout the world, they can't wait to dig in and win. All of their life and their parent's lives, they have been repressed by government and denied freedom of enterprise. Once here, they are like a hungry child in an ice cream store. While many of us who were born here and have never known anything but freedom of opportunity wait for the government or others to care for us, they go around us like an Indy 500 car on a dirt road. They arrive on our shores full of dreams, enthusiasm, plans, determination and a strong work ethic. They study harder, work smarter, work longer and bingo, their dreams come true. They become our best doctors, teachers, engineers, computer experts and entrepreneurs. Their attitude is "give me freedom - I'll take care of everything else!"

How about this for a success story: Intel Corp. was started by a Hungarian immigrant. The market value of Intel today is more than the combined market values of General Motors, Ford, Chrysler and U.S. Steel. Intel is a reality today because of freedom, law and order and the "incentive" system.

I was in Atlanta, Georgia as a guest attending Hal and Susan Gooch's Free Enterprise Day convention. The taxi driver taking our party to the airport was from Bangladesh. He was asked how the U.S. compared to Bangladesh. He responded, "You cannot compare the two, the U.S. is the greatest country in the world. There is so much opportunity here. In Bangladesh, if you went to work for $5.00 per hour, you would die still making $5.00 per hour, but in America, in 6 months you could be a manager and in a few years build a mansion." Thank you cabbie, we could not have said it better.

The fact that you are reading this book means you wish to be a cut above the average. And the only limit on your potential for success is what you impose upon yourself. You may not be able to do anything about the economy, the stock market, bank failures or wars, but you can control your attitude, your enthusiasm, commitment, determination and work habits. If you control these things, you will achieve greatness.

There are many people who do not try to do better due to their belief that one person cannot have a major impact. Oh yeah! What about Lincoln - Helen Keller - Pasteur - Mother Teresa - Michelangelo - Einstein - Roosevelt and Reagan? How about Bill Gates and Michael Dell? How about the Yagers and the Goochs who started with nothing and today manage thousands of emerging success stories? If you think one person can't make a difference, think about this. Would it make a difference if you

- took one player from a basketball team?
- took one runner from a relay team?
- took one wheel from your car?
- took one roof tile from your roof?
- took one piece of sheet rock from your ceiling?
- removed one exterior door from your home?
- lost one eye?
- had only one leg?
- lost one member of your family?

The fact is one person makes a tremendous difference. The amount of difference depends on you. Life is like a parade. You can be one of the crowd waving – or – you can be the one riding and waving back! It's up to you! I once read that, "if you care more than others think is wise, if you risk more than others think is safe, dream more than others think is practical and expect more than others think is possible – you will enjoy more than most can imagine." If you truly want to improve your life and the lives of people around you, including your family members, then begin right now by living these 13 keys. Establish the habit of reading this little book every week. Establish the habit of reading other good personal improvement, success-oriented books. Establish the goal you want to achieve and don't let anything discourage you. It has been stated that the person you will be in five years will be determined by the books you read, the tapes you listen to and the type of people you associate with.

Always remember that God endowed you with the ability to gloriously provide for your family. Yes! You can become a millionaire. I promise you, if you live the principles outlined in this book, you will break the success code!

## Winners Versus Losers

Winners are always part of the answer - Losers are part of the problem!

Winners always have a program - Losers an excuse!

Winners always say "I'll do it" - Losers say that's not my job!

Winners always see an answer for every problem - Losers see a problem in every answer!

Winners say it may be difficult, but it's possible - Losers say it may be possible, but it's too difficult.

# One Of My Goals

If I can make you laugh...or cry tears of joy...or make you think...or make you spring into action for good...then I have done us both a favor.

One of my goals with this book is to disturb you. In essence, to plow up the inner thoughts of your mind, to turn over the soil of your heart. What you need is new growth, intellectually, psychologically, and in your level of expectancy. Growth follows a disturbance – the seeds we plant grow best in soil that has been turned and broken. From the ashes of failure (disturbance) great achievements arise. Our greatest knowledge is attained from experiencing our biggest mistakes (disturbance).

Some of the most beautiful and useful artwork is performed by master potters. Making pottery is just like molding your own life. You cannot work clay into a valuable article without pressure being applied. The potter can spin his clay until it dries up and nothing will happen until he takes his hands and applies the pressure that will mold the clay into his chosen piece of art.

Molding your life into an effective performance machine that will utilize your many talents, will require that you apply pressure much like the potter. Until you challenge yourself to do your best, you will not experience the pressure that creates growth.

# Have An Attitude

My first job was selling newspapers on street corners in Little Rock, Arkansas, at age 12. I had an attitude! The attitude that I must be the very best paper salesman they had. I later worked for Mr. Deb Howard, who had a brahman cattle operation. I had an attitude, the attitude that I had to be the very best cattle helper he ever had. He said I was. I worked for Doyle Venable at Venable Lumber Company. I had an attitude. The attitude that I must be the very best employee he ever had. The best at cleaning the yard, the office, stacking lumber, loading cement, unloading box cars, delivering truck loads of lumber, sheet rock, then in sales. Then, manager of the paint department estimating costs of homes, etc., etc. He said I was the best he ever had. No matter what it was, selling newspapers, working on the ranch or at the lumber yard, I knew I was the best and needed to prove it for my own self-esteem. It was this same attitude that made me succeed as an insurance agent, sales manager, corporate executive and founder of five life insurance holding companies.

If there is a secret to success, that's it! Have an attitude. The attitude that you are the best and work your tail off to prove it. There is no substitute for knowing you can outwork and outperform everyone else. Most success stories do not happen accidentally. Success is intentional. Know what you want, do everything to be the best at everything you do on your climb up the ladder. Read, study and prepare yourself for the success you desire and it will happen. Have an attitude!

## Nothing Comes Easy

Freedom of enterprise offers us many wonderful opportunities. The freedom to "try" is a priceless advantage that few people in the world enjoy. However, freedom also brings responsibilities and risks. This world of risk and reward seldom delivers a bed of roses without strong challenges. Most people, on their journey to success, were grasped by the nape of the neck and tossed around like a rag doll in a turbulent world. They were slammed to the earth, kicked and dragged through the mud before the system finally surrendered to a positive thinking, committed and determined person. You will be tested and sometimes brutally, but you can win.

One of the absolute necessities for the average person to succeed is determination. Many people have been close to the big breakthrough that would have propelled them to great success only to give up. Anyone can quit, but it takes a person of real character and determination to succeed or deserve success.

## The Freeport McMoRan Story…

…the multi-billion dollar company that almost wasn't. In approximately 1972, three men pooled all their resources and knowledge to drill for oil in south Texas. In spite of their enthusiasm and confidence, their early drillings were extremely disappointing. As so often happens, their early failures proved once again that nothing comes easy. Jim Bob Moffett, Mack Rankin and W. Kennon McWilliams decided not to quit. They scraped together just enough money to make one more attempt. They understood that if this drilling ended with the same results, that it would be the end of their dreams. This one last drilling would be a do or die effort. If it failed, they would have to fold their tent, put out the fire and everyone go their separate ways. In order to make this last drilling, it required faith, courage, total commitment and absolute determination.

They were rewarded for not quitting by a gusher that enabled them to prove a vast new field of oil and gas. From this discovery grew Freeport McMoRan Inc. This giant company today employs thousands worldwide and has created fortunes for thousands of employees and investors. One more dry hole or the decision not to drill one more time, would have been disastrous for its future employees and investors.

# Broke But Not Beaten

I remember when I first started out as an insurance agent, I experienced fairly good success from the very beginning. I was working on a commission only basis as did most new agents. I thought this was going to be easy. It seemed like out of nowhere and for no apparent reason the dreaded "sales slump" hit with a vengeance. I couldn't have given my product away, much less talk someone into paying for it. I went thirteen weeks without making a sale. That is ¼ of a year without making a dime. I was living in a two room garage apartment by the railroad tracks in Ada, Oklahoma. The winter was very cold and the wind would blow 30-40 miles per hour. The wind would blow around the windows enough to make the curtains inside stand out. With no income, I was behind in my rent, utilities, telephone and car payment. They cut off my telephone and repossessed my car. I hocked my typewriter which I needed to type lead letters to prospects and I hocked my wrist watch. I remember I got $4.00 for my watch. I was broke but not beaten.

I picked up pop bottles along the road for 2 cents each to buy milk for the baby and ate navy beans for breakfast, lunch and dinner, in order to survive as a new insurance agent. During those tough times, I sought out others who were succeeding. Generally, they thought I wanted to borrow money, but I was seeking knowledge. I told them, "don't give me part of your earnings, teach me how you earned it." Was this the time to quit and as some would say, go get a real job? Most people would say yes!

Not once did I even consider quitting. In fact, I knew in the very depths of my heart that I could succeed. Not only did I not consider quitting, I was creating my goal and plan to someday start my own Life Insurance Company during this horrible sales slump. Can you imagine that? My dreams were bigger than my problems, bigger than my challenges, bigger than anything trying to defeat me. I learned that one person's two cent throw away bottles was another person's milk for his child.

I was determined to do whatever it took to make it. I was feeding my mind by reading two books during this time – Napolean Hills, "Think and Grow Rich" and W. Clement Stone's, "The Success System That Never Fails." I committed to doing what these books taught me and never looked back.

During the fourteenth week, I finally made a sale and then another one and another one. Never again did I experience a sales slump. I had been tested severely and I passed the test. You can pass the test too, or you can quit. It all depends on how badly you wish to succeed and how determined you are.

I discovered that success was not a secret but a disciplined formula. I have given you the formula in this book; it is up to you to provide the discipline. I am teaching you what I learned. You are holding the blueprint in your hands.

Frequently, you will hear a person admiringly referred to as an over-achiever, due to their excellent performance. You cannot over-achieve, you cannot do something you can't do. However, you can do things you didn't think you could do. The problem is most people "under-expect." You can sell yourself or others short.

You have to go all out to achieve great goals. You can be the fastest person alive but if you enter a race and run carefully in order to avoid any possible injury, you are not going to win! Whatever you wish to achieve, you must go all out. Freeport McMoRan Inc. exists today because Jim Bob Moffett, Mack

Rankin and W. Kennon McWilliams went all out, laid it all on the line and burned their bridges behind them. Their courage, commitment and determination today feeds many thousands of people who depend on this great company for their livelihood. Thank you, gentlemen, for your courage and foresight. Bill Gates, the CEO of Microsoft, stated on "Larry King Live" that one of the keys to success was, massive and immediate action. I have always liked the way the Indianapolis 500 begins the race with these simple words: "Ladies and gentlemen, start your engines." We should repeat those words every morning, followed by massive and immediate action.

## A Wagon Dog!

In 1974, I had a business appointment with a very successful entrepreneur in Indianapolis, Indiana. After meeting for approximately one-half hour, he wanted to know all about my background and experiences. He listened intently and then called his son in to participate in the rest of the meeting. He told his son that he finally found what he was wanting to show him. He said, "This man is 'A Wagon Dog'." I wasn't sure how to take that, but I smiled and continued our meeting.

When the meeting was over, I asked him what he meant about my being a 'wagon dog.' He said that as the people were settling the country and heading out west by wagon, that most families had a dog that went along on the trip. As they went across the country, the wagon dog had to become the best dog around. He had to fight off every dog in every little settlement, fight wolves, coyotes, bears and protect his master's family and property. He said, "I have always told my son that every once in a while you will run across a wagon dog in business. You're the first one I've been able to show my son." No one ever paid me a higher compliment.

I have often thought since then that real winners in life are like the wagon dogs. There are constant challenges, road blocks, disappointments, dogs in every settlement that have to be avoided or fought and just like the wagon dogs, the truly motivated, committed, winner prevails.

## The Hal & Susan Gooch Story

The success of the Amway Corporation is one of the greatest success stories in the history of the world. In 1959, Rich DeVos and Jay Van Andel started the company in the basement of their homes. Today, it is a multi-billion dollar company with 3 million independent entrepreneurs worldwide. Approximately 35 years ago Uncle Ron Gooch convinced Hal and Susan Gooch that they had an opportunity to improve their life with a career with Amway. With nothing but faith, enthusiasm and determination, they began a new career.

That one decision has improved the lives of thousands of Americans and thousands in foreign countries. Once a year, Hal and Susan hold a Free Enterprise Day Convention for their distributors. The only place in Atlanta big enough to hold them is the Georgia Dome. Thirty to forty thousand distributors descend upon Atlanta and it ranks in the top ten Atlanta conventions annually. These people are merely invited. They come from all over and pay their own way to Atlanta, including hotel, meals and $110.00 per ticket to attend the three-day event. The Goochs won't ever tell them who the speakers will be or the entertainment. They come knowing that it will be unbelievable and it always is.

Another reason they come is because the Goochs have helped

make many of them millionaires. Many more are on their way to becoming millionaires and thousands more are learning they can be. The Goochs are prototype Americans. They began their career at ground zero and experienced every hardship and disappointment you can imagine. Most people would have quit, but the Goochs had the faith and courage to persevere. Today, they live a life that only kings and queens can dream of and they deserve it.

They generously share their wealth and go all out to help others do what the Goochs have done. They believe in God! They believe in America! They believe in freedom! And they believe in people!

## Blessings

Most human beings have been blessed. They were endowed with enthusiasm, natural intelligence, the ability to dream, think and plan, commitment and determination, the ability to learn and solve problems, the ability to love and be loved, the ability to entertain and appreciate being entertained. With these endowments, what more could you possibly ask for? You have been given the ability and talents to achieve anything and enjoy everything.

However, as we mature, we allow negative thinking to gradually take over our minds, our hearts and our bodies. We begin to dwell on what's not right with our lives, what we don't have that others do, make excuses for our failures, expect others or the government to provide for us and become professional whiners. We drink too much, we smoke too much, we eat too much and lay around too much. Soon, too many people start looking for excitement in their lives in all the wrong places.

Some eventually turn to God for help and pray that God will

solve their problems. One should not ask God to solve their problems but pray that God will help them remember all the blessings already bestowed upon them and help them re-establish those talents and abilities so that they can then whip any problem they have on their own through positive thinking and positive action.

Negative thinking is the primary tool of the devil – all you have to do to destroy a human being is turn their thinking negative. Do you think God could have created all the heavens and the earth, all the animals and all the fish and topped it all off with the creation of man and woman by thinking negatively? God was thinking positively, enthusiastically, intelligently, determinedly. He had a master plan which he dreamed up and committed himself to complete. He gave it all to man and blessed him with the same abilities to think positively, creatively, commit to good over evil and add to the assets bestowed upon man.

Since then, man has achieved much greatness. Every achievement has been the result of positive thinking and utilization of the other endowments granted each of us.

Name one great achievement as the result of negative thoughts, whining, griping, stealing or laziness.

Most all of man's problems, other than health or natural disasters, since the beginning of time, have been brought on themselves by negative thinking and expectations.

## God Has Endowed You!

Throughout this book, you have noticed I have kept reminding you that, "God has endowed you with the ability to gloriously provide for your family."

I have done this in order that it might serve as a sub-conscience alarm clock. Wake up! Wake up! Wake up!

Millions of people go through life as if they never realize they have all the talents needed to become gloriously successful. The vast majority of people have the same mental and physical capabilities that big-time Winners enjoy. The difference in people is in how they use their talents and recognize the talents they possess.

Except for those whom are born with mental and physical birth defects, do you honestly believe that God endowed you with less capabilities than most others? Absolutely not! You have the God-given talents to achieve almost anything that you want.

There is unbelievable power within you, when you suddenly realize the capabilities you have within you. If you wish to give an excuse for not achieving more, there is always plenty to choose from. But, the excuse that God gave you too little talent, is not one of them. Wake up…and say "thank you God for the talents you bestowed upon me."

Recognize your talents. Appreciate your talents, believe in your talents and utilize your talents. Financial success and personal happiness is yours for the taking. The "cup of happiness" is available to each of us. Some people never touch the cup of happiness, others sip from it with great apprehension, but winners drink mightily from the cup. Winners know that you cannot empty the cup of happiness, because it is refilled at the same rate you drink from it. It is up to you whether you wish to be a sipper or a hearty drinker. Whenever you accept the fact that the ability to achieve is within you, then you will agree that…yes, you can become a millionaire! Would you rather say, "I'm glad I did it" or "If only I had?"

If there is something that you can do to improve life for others, develop a latent talent, create opportunity for the needy or unemployed, motivate, train or make them laugh, help a negative thinker become positive, a small thinker think big, give hope where despair resides, you must do it! For your sake and their sake, you must do it! It is our duty – the cost of the ticket for this wonderful ride we are on in America.

Kevin Ahart, age 17

## Pot of Gold

"You" are the pot of gold at the end of the rainbow! You and I have been told all of our lives that there is a pot of gold at the end of the rainbow. Sounds nice, doesn't it? It's a statement of hope. Something to dream about and lift our spirits. Somewhat similar to "the meek shall inherit the earth." Somewhat heady stuff, huh? Hey! If those statements bring you comfort, here's a couple more… You could win the lottery someday or a rich uncle may leave you a fortune. There! Do you feel better now? Anything to make you feel good. We aim to please! But wait, don't go out and buy that new lazy boy rocker just yet. Statistics, those dreaded statistics, are always interrupting our simple-minded dreams and prove that none of these things are likely to happen to you. You mean, I'm more likely to be struck by lightning, than I am to have riches fall in my lap? Yep, 'fraid so! But, that's not bad news, in fact, it's good news. Now you don't have to waste your time making sure you're home when the lottery director calls.

The real good news is that you have been walking around with a pot of gold all of your adult life. You're it! Your body, your heart, your mind, is a vessel that can create its own gold throughout your life. You don't need to wait until God creates a rainbow, He put the rainbow in "you." You are unique! There's not another one just like you anywhere in the world. There's no limit to what you can do. Once you realize this, then you truly begin to live. Let the world see the rainbow radiating from you. What are all those vivid colors, protruding from your chest, arching into the heavens? It's a rainbow and look, you are the pot of gold at the end.

When my father was a young boy, he was working in the field with his dad. After a brief shower, a beautiful rainbow appeared with the very end (or beginning) only a few yards away. My dad ran and stood in the beautiful bouquet of colors, descending from the heavens. It was a thrilling moment for him and his dad. Not surprisingly, he found no pot of gold. Unbeknownst to him at the time, he was it! He was the "pot of gold" at the end of the rainbow.

## Success Versus Wealth

Yes, there is a lot of despicable behavior by a lot of people, including so-called leaders. The reported lying and illicit sex from the White House in epidemic proportions sends a message to everyone that it's okay, cool and acceptable. Even more despicable is the "spin line" from the president's supporters that it's expected. I heard one of the president's supporters say that if you ran everybody out of Washington that committed adultery and then lied about it, there would be no one left in Washington.

This statement is a vast exaggeration. If you listen to them, you get the impression that Washington D.C. makes Sodom and Gomorrah seem like wicked city trainees.

Admittedly, there are far too many people, from the highest places to the lowest places, engaging in behavior your mother would not approve of: politicians, business leaders, preachers, blue collar workers, teachers, all the way to street people who participate in illicit sex, cheating, stealing, embezzling and other forms of moral decadence.

This behavior is wrong! This behavior is damaging and costly to all of society, including themselves. What good is it in the long run if you become financially successful, but you're morally bankrupt? True happiness comes with success and honor. There can be no honor with low morals. Honor doesn't live in the same house with immorality. In truth, there is no success where immorality defeats honor. There is such a thing as "just" having a lot of money or position and no other redeeming value.

Immorality is not okay! Cheating, stealing, lying is not okay! Any victory obtained by cheating is not worth having. This is true whether it's a kid winning an athletic event or a politician winning a race for mayor, senator or president. Any ill-gotten gain will turn rotten on you in the end.

However, in spite of improper behavior by others from the back alleys to the White House, there's good news for you.

You can be highly successful, moral, ethical and a person of high honor. "If" you do your best to live the 13 attributes in the "Profile of a Winner," you will make it. A person who has goals, ethics, enthusiasm, determination, good work habits and a strong commitment cannot be denied. Yes, you can become a millionaire!

Don't allow the improper behavior of others to influence you or discourage you. There's a fight going on out there for success – there's a fight going on out there for right and wrong – there's a fight going on out there to determine whether morality or immorality will rule society – get in the fight and help us win for "success" for "right" and for "morality."

Get in the fight for the sake of your children, for the sake of the less fortunate and for the sake of America and freedom.

Do not ever attempt to compete with lying, cheating, stealing or any illicit behavior. Your competition is yourself and the temptations that flow your way in the natural flow of life.

It is up to society, including you, to defeat the above behavior by exposure and the rule of law. Real winners, real honest to goodness, moral, hard-working, goal-driven Americans say "No" to temptations to stray from the "right" path.

My former boss, the late D.N. "Nick" Pope used to jokingly say, "I can withstand anything but temptation." He then would launch into a lecture on the necessity of avoiding inappropriate temptations if one was to enjoy success with honor! Thank you, Mr. Pope, for your leadership and example.

# Success Gems

1. Yes! You can become a millionaire.
2. The road to success is less traveled!
3. Ideas work - if you do!
4. Dreams come true when you are wide-awake!
5. "Never, never, never give up!" – *Prime Minister, Winston Churchill*
6. Action speaks louder than - inaction!
7. Success comes in cans – failure in can'ts!
8. Success is spelled "p-e-r-s-e-v-e-r-a-n-c-e."
9. It wasn't raining when Noah built the Ark.  Plan ahead!
10. Greatness has a price – EFFORT!
11. No alibis!
12. You can't start tomorrow to succeed today!
13. Lady luck shines brightest around seven AM!
14. God gives every bird his worm – he does not throw it in his nest! – *Swedish Proverb*
15. Your happiness is your responsibility!
16. Limits are generally self-imposed!
17. Eagles always fly alone!
18. Success is more attitude than aptitude.
19. It's what we learn after we think we know it all that counts!
20. The strong laugh at challenges.
21. Work habits determine success!
22. Success formula: Dream - Risk - Expect!
23. Problems create opportunities!
24. Opportunity knocks ever so softly!
25. Opportunity always comes dressed in work clothes!
26. The gift of enthusiasm keeps on giving!

27. In America, no healthy person has to stay poor!
28. Goals work two ways: You work for them and they work on you!
29. The difference in mediocrity and greatness is slight!
30. Happiness is not pleasure – its victory!
31. The finish line for some is the starting line for others.
32. Live your life so you can look ahead with enthusiasm and look back with pride.
33. You don't have to be a star to perform out of this world!
34. Burn your bridges and you have to go forward!
35. A person's dreams should not die until the person dies!
36. Adversity is the surest teacher!
37. One cannot over-achieve, one can under-expect, one can sell oneself short.
38. You don't need an earth-shattering idea to succeed, you need earth-shattering performance and service.
39. Vision has nothing to do with eyesight.
40. Dreams don't come true…while dreaming.
41. The customer is always right…is wrong, but they should be made to feel they are right.
42. There is nothing of lesser value than a capable person with a poor attitude.
43. You can't change the past, but you're not past making changes.
44. A goal should make you proud.

# Author's Note

Do others see greater potential in you than you see? I thought so! You know what? The others are right. You can do better than you think you can.

It is my sincere desire that this book will help inspire you and lead you to greater success. By design, this is a short book. I wanted something you can read within an hour or so and then read it again every week until you know it by heart. I wrote it from my heart. Unlike most authors, I did no research on this book. I just sat down and wrote it based solely on my life's experiences. I lived it!

I began accumulating knowledge of people and learning from them during my first job, selling newspapers on street corners, then subsequently; ranch work, working at a lumber company, as an insurance agent and ultimately, founder and chairman of five successful insurance companies.

I have had the privilege of working hand in hand with many of America's best leaders in business, academia and sports. All of those leaders utilized and epitomized the principles outlined in this book.

## Be A Carrier And Infect Others

-Be a carrier of positive thinking

-Be a carrier of happiness

-Be a carrier of total commitment

-Be a carrier of determination

-Be a carrier of enthusiasm

-Be a carrier of honesty

Empty the hospitals by being a carrier of positive "diseases" worth fighting for.

## Are you scared?

Good! I have never known a highly successful person who was not scared when they first started. You're in good company. I heard someone say once that you weigh fear in ounces but regrets in pounds.

## According To A Recent Survey of Successful Entrepreneurs
### By: Inc. Magazine

A. Seventy-six percent said, "it was the extraordinary execution of an ordinary idea that caused their success rather than an unusual or extraordinary idea."

> *Translation - You don't need an earth shattering idea to succeed - you need earth-shattering performance and service.*

B. Ninety-five percent see entrepreneurs, not CEOs of large corporations as the heroes of American business.

> *Translation - You will receive the highest level of*

*respect and admiration as a successful independent entrepreneur.*

C. Eighty-five percent said cash flow and funding were their company's biggest hurdles.
*Translation - Most of today's business leaders started with little financing. There is hope for you, too.*

## Leadership Qualities

Good leaders are good people. Good leaders are moral people. Leaders lead! Those who drive, intimidate, harass and threaten to increase performance are not leaders but dictators. We all know what happens to all dictators over time. An organization, whether private, public, political or a sports franchise is only as good as the people and how they react to upper management. Dictators often experience short term bursts of higher performance but sustained improvement requires leadership. Good leaders use common sense. They know not to do things to their team members which they disliked when it was done to them. ("Do unto others as you would have others do unto you.") They always do those things which they appreciated and admired in their own leaders. They deal with their people from a principle of integrity. A leader must be believable. They understand everyone's need for motivation and knowledge. They are fair and promote based on performance and ability as opposed to favoritism.

It takes people of character to be good leaders. You cannot purchase character. You develop and earn it. It would be nice, but we cannot put old heads on young shoulders. To manage others you must first prove you can manage yourself. Your outward accomplishments will generally match your inward growth. If you're the biggest pig at the trough, does that make you the leader? No! Just a big old sloppy selfish bullying hog.

A good leader needs good wisdom and wisdom comes one action at a time. Good leaders concern themselves with fixing the problem, not the blame. Leaders liberally disburse compliments whenever they're due. Have you ever received too many compliments? You don't need leadership to take a crowd where they naturally want to go. You need leadership to steer people on a path that is right. The easy path is generally not the right path. That's why we need leaders. Leaders ask a lot of questions such as, "what do you think?" The most productive question asked by great leaders is "what is your advice?" To be a good leader you must learn to think for yourself but not of yourself.

The view is always better at the top of the mountain, but the winds of change and challenge always blow harder the higher you go.

Leaders never let up. Leaders know that if you let up when things are going well, the result will be the same as turning off the engines when your plane has leveled off. Don't do it! If leaders let up, Amway, Wal-Mart, Microsoft, Dell, Inc., Freeport McMoRan, would not be the giants they are today.

Those loyal to what "is" make good managers and supervisors – the shapers of what "might be" make good leaders.

## List of Winners With Whom The Author Has Worked Closely Over The Last 35 Years*

Tom Landry, Former Coach of the Dallas Cowboys
Darrell K. Royal, Former Coach Texas Longhorns
Frank Broyles, Former Coach Arkansas Razorbacks
Bob DeVaney, Former Coach Nebraska Cornhuskers
Hayden Fry, Coach Iowa Hawkeyes
Johnny Majors, Former Coach Tennessee Volunteers
Chris Schenkel, ABC Sportscaster
C. James McCormick, Former Chairman, American Truckers Association, former Chairman, Fellowship of Christian Athletes and Principal Owner of Innisbrook & Tamarron Golf Resorts
Charles Thone, Former Congressman & Gov. of Nebraska
Winfield Dunn, Former Governor of Tennessee
John Ryan, Former President University of Indiana
Earl Butz, Former Agri/Econ Professor - Purdue University & U.S. Secretary of Agriculture
Capt. Eugene Cernan, Astronaut (2 moon missions)
Richard Fulton, Former Congressman & Mayor of Nashville, TN
D.N. Pope, Founder of National Foundation Life and Farm & Ranch Life

## Motivational Trainers

Zig Ziglar.... Charlie "Tremendous" Jones... J. Douglas Edwards

*I have only listed those who are well known to the public. There are another 40 or 50 who are lesser known but who are just as wonderful and capable who served on various Boards

of Directors with me or whom I've worked with in the past. Remember, a son of sharecroppers was able to surround himself with these leaders. The reason was they believed in my integrity, enthusiasm, positive attitude, commitment, goals and determination. Surround yourself with the best and you'll become the best. We all have the tendency to live up to or down to the quality of friends and associates we have around us.

My special thanks to hundreds of associates I have been privileged to have around me through the years. Many of them went on to form their own companies and enjoyed great success. I will not list them because I could fill several pages and I sure wouldn't want to leave someone out. They know who they are.

## About the Author

Wayne Ahart was one of nine children born and raised in rural Arkansas. He grew up poor but proud in a time and place that was still struggling to overcome the crippling effects of the Depression. He was taught to believe in America and the vast opportunities available to all. He learned that good work habits, strong ethics, enthusiasm and determination were the keys to a successful life. After selling newspapers on street corners and working for a lumber company, he became a life insurance agent at age 22. Wayne set a personal goal of forming his own life insurance company and becoming a millionaire by age 35. He achieved both goals by age 33 and went on to become founder and chairman of five successful companies in five states. Wayne's achievements have come from following the success formula outlined in this book and utilizing the talents with which each of us are born.

"The best way to say 'I love you' to your spouse and children is Life insurance. It's the gift that keeps on saying 'I Love You,' long after you're gone."
							*-Wayne Ahart*

"The best way to instill love of country and respect for law is to demonstrate it by your own life."
							*-Wayne Ahart*

# EPILOGUE
## Tax Incentive System versus Disincentive System

Would you start a business and design a marketing plan whereby your customers had to pay more per item, the more they bought? In essence, a disincentive to increase their purchases from your business? If they could go to your competition and receive volume discounts whereby the more they bought, the less they paid per item, where do you think they would go to do business?

How about a system of paying your employee's less the more they work? Do you think they would work for you or a competitor who paid them more, the more they worked?

The U.S. Federal income tax system creates such disincentives – the more you make, the higher percentage you pay, i.e. punishment for doing better. Retirees on Social Security are punished when they earn above a certain amount, thereby causing millions of potential producers to sit on their hands. A tax system should create an incentive for people to earn more, create more, save more and invest more by decreasing the percentage paid as your income rises while increasing total receipts.

The federal government doesn't pay its bills in "percentages" but with total receipts. Therefore, the U.S. should motivate citizens with an incentive to create more income. The government would then increase total receipts, by decreasing the tax percentage as citizens climb the income ladder.

No rule should ever punish a person for making something good happen. How much better off would the poor be, if ordinary citizens were encouraged to start new businesses or expand existing ones creating more jobs? New or expanded businesses buy other products that strengthen the economy and cause other businesses to hire more people. These people pay more taxes and the businesses pay more taxes.

If incentive doesn't work, then why do the countries with free markets feed and protect the rest of the world?

The current discussion of a flat tax system would be a vast improvement over the present system. However, a greater improvement would be a system that rewards greater and greater success, by reducing the scale of tax payments, the higher the income goes. In essence, you pay more by paying less. A simple example: A taxpayer earning $100,000.00 with a tax rate of 20% would pay his government $20,000. If he can increase his income to $200,000, he would qualify for the lower rate of say 15%. But, he would pay his government $30,000. The government has increased total receipts while the taxpayer keeps $10,000 more of his earnings which he will use to invest or spend, which in turn creates more taxes for the government. In my opinion, the very best tax system would be no tax at all on income from any U.S. citizen, corporation or partnership. Encourage every American to earn, save and invest all the money he can. A sales tax should be charged for every transaction in goods or services except food. A consumption tax assures that all Americans will rightfully participate in the financing of their government, but the wealthy would pay by far the most since they spend and invest the most. Non-U.S. citizens and corporations should pay a tax on all earnings they take out of the country.

The most nonsensical tax that should be immediately eliminated, or at the very least altered, is what I call the "death tax" or the "last bite tax." The government calls it the "estate tax."

Picture this! You have spent a lifetime achieving, accumulating and saving. You have enjoyed some success and you're proud that you have acquired enough assets to pass along to your beloved family. It's your money, you earned it and you're going to divide it up among those you love. No! No! No! The last bite belongs to the IRS! How ridiculous for you to assume that your achievements should belong to your heirs! You do not have the right to die without punishment. Therefore, the government will punish you for dying by appropriating "one last bite" from your living efforts. The "death tax" strikes a mighty blow against your spouse and children.

It's important to remember that every step of the way you have already paid taxes on every dollar you accumulated. Every dollar you have saved is "after tax" dollars. Every penny of investment income your savings earned has also been taxed. You have paid taxes on everything you ever bought or rented. You have paid taxes on everything you have ever eaten, worn, lived in, or driven.

Now, upon your death, the death of an achiever, a contributor to society, what possible right does the black gloved hand of government have to what's left of what you earned? It's nonsense – kill it and kill it fast!

In the meantime, until we elect enough courageous and fair-minded representatives to kill the "death tax," at least amend it.

Many heirs, such as farmers or property owners, are forced to sell what their benefactor worked to accumulate just to create the cash to pay the "last tax bite."

Until this unfair tax is eliminated entirely, the tax code should be amended to require taxes be paid whenever the assets are sold as opposed to being transferred through death. One should not have to pay taxes on a growing tree but when the tree is harvested for lumber. Thousands of farmers' heirs have been forced to sell the farm to pay taxes when they should have been paying taxes on its operations and the "death tax" on its eventual sale.

I have included this section to illustrate the incentive system. The incentive system is the driving force that has made America and its' citizens world leaders in production, technology and military security. Also, I urge you to send this book to your Congressional and Senatorial representatives. Urge them to support improving the tax system from a system of punishment to a system that encourages and rewards ability, desire and initiative. There would be far fewer poor people in our country if we rewarded risk takers in ventures that provide employment and expanded opportunities.

Sam Walton learned you make more by charging less and selling more. Congress, are you listening?

*Wayne's father, S.H. Ahart, Arkansas. He was a Watkins Products salesman circa 1940's.*

*My brothers, Tom and Dean, circa 1945. Arkansas.*

Wayne is catching, brother Bill is batting. Arkansas, approximately age 10. Circa 1950.

*Wayne Ahart on far left at Venable Lumber Co., North Little Rock, Arkansas (age 18). 1958.*

*At right, Wayne Ahart (age 35), President and Chairman, Investors Trust Assurance Company, Indiana. Circa 1975.*

*Below, Wayne's Mom, Dad and siblings. Wayne is in the center, approximately age 19, circa 1959. Arkansas.*

*Wayne and D.N. "Nick" Pope, approximately age 40, Canada. Circa 1980.*

*Below, Wayne on Corporate Director C. James McCormick's yacht. Approximately age 42. Circa 1982.*

*Wayne presenting award to Don Byrd, Future Security Life Insurance Co., Austin, Texas, approximately age 43, circa 1983.*

*Wayne with Coach Royal and Edith at Austin, Texas, approximately age 43, circa 1983.*

*Chairman Ahart, Austin, Texas, age 43, circa 1983.*

*Chairman Ahart presenting Man of the Year award to Kenny Tobey. Austin, Texas, approximately age 43, circa 1983.*

*Wayne meeting insurance official, Beijing, China, age 44. Circa 1984.*

*Wayne visiting a commune in China, approximately age 44. Circa 1984.*

Above, Wayne's cowboy hat on Russian soldier in Moscow, circa 1984.

Right, Wayne meeting Russian Minister of Insurance, Moscow. Approximately age 44, circa 1984.

Below, Wayne visiting a group of school girls in Moscow. Cowboy hat and boots were a big hit. Age 44, circa 1984.

*YES! You Can Become a Millionaire*

*Above, Wayne and brother Tom. First airplane, Cessna 421, approximately age 45, Mexico. Circa 1985.*

*Below, Wayne with Willie Nelson, Austin, Texas. Approximately age 50, circa 1990.*

*Above, Wayne Ahart (age 55) with Captain Eugene Cernan, left, and Coach Hayden Fry, right, both corporate directors. Austin, Texas, circa 1995.*

*Below, golfing with Tom Landry and C. James McCormick, Austin, Texas. Approximately age 59. My son, Kevin, second from left - a great golfer and professional singer. Circa 1999.*

*Son Chris Ahart receives his University of Texas law degree from William Rogers, Jr., former Dean of the University of Texas Law School, currently serving as President. Chris' law degree compliments his accounting degree and CPA certification, 2002.*

*Above, My son Doug and family by a Beech jet he flies, Austin, Texas, circa 2004.*

*Below, Wayne and brother Tom, approximately age 64, circa 2004.*

*Above, Wayne and daughter Deborah Berman, co-owner Bazbeaux Pizza, Indianapolis. Approximately age 65, circa 2005.*

*Right, Mom Ahart, Arkansas, age 90. She will be 92, October 31, 2007.*

*Below, My friends, Coach Darrell Royal and Reverend Rex Johnson. Coach is a former director with Wayne. Circa 2006.*